QABALAH

IN THE SAME SERIES

Principles of Acupuncture *Angela Hicks*
Principles of Aikido *Paul Wildish*
Principles of Alexander Technique *Jeremy Chance*
Principles of Aromatherapy *Cathy Hopkins*
Principles of Art Therapies *Daniel Brown*
Principles of Buddhism *Kulananda*
Principles of Chinese Herbal Medicine *John Hicks*
Principles of Chinese Medicine *Angela Hicks*
Principles of Colonic Irrigation *Jillie Collings*
Principles of Colour Healing *Ambika Wauters and Gerry Thompson*
Principles of the Enneagram *Karen Webb*
Principles of Fasting *Leon Chaitow*
Principles of Feng Shui *Simon Brown*
Principles of Hypnotherapy *Vera Peiffer*
Principles of Jungian Spirituality *Vivianne Crowley*
Principles of Kinesiology *Maggie la Tourelle and Anthea Courtenay*
Principles of Meditation *Christina Feldman*
Principles of Native American Spirituality *Dennis Renault and Timothy Freke*
Principles of NLP *Joseph O'Connor and Ian McDermott*
Principles of Numerology *Sonia Ducie*
Principles of Nutritional Therapy *Linda Lazarides*
Principles of Paganism *Vivianne Crowley*
Principles of Palmistry *Lillian Verner Bonds*
Principles of Past Life Therapy *Julie Hall*
Principles of Your Psychic Potential *David Lawson*
Principles of Psychotherapy *Brice Avery*
Principles of Reflexology *Nicola Hall*
Principles of Reiki *Kajsa Krishni Borang*
Principles of Self-Healing *David Lawson*
Principles of Shamanism *Leo Rutherford*
Principles of Shiatsu *Chris Jarmey*
Principles of Stress Management *Vera Peiffer*
Principles of Tai Chi *Paul Brecher*
Principles of Tarot *Evelyne and Terry Donaldson*
Principles of Vibrational Healing *Clare Harvey*
Principles of Wicca *Vivianne Crowley*
Principles of Yoga *Sara Martin*

QABALAH

AMBER JAYANTI

Thorsons

IN LOVING MEMORY OF MY MOTHER, FLORENCE
NOVEMBER 18TH, 1910–MARCH 18TH, 1992
'UNTO YOU PARADISE IS OPENED, THE TREE OF LIFE IS PLANTED.'
ETHIOPIC BOOK OF ENOCH

Thorsons
An Imprint of HarperCollins*Publishers*
77–85 Fulham Palace Road,
Hammersmith, London W6 8JB

Published by Thorsons 1999

3 5 7 9 10 8 6 4

© Amber Jayanti 1999

Amber Jayanti asserts the moral right to
be identified as the author of this work

A catalogue record for this book
is available from the British Library

ISBN 0 7225 3680 1

Printed and bound in Great Britain by
Caledonian International Book Manufacturing Ltd, Glasgow

CONTENTS

Acknowledgements   vii
'To Receive'   ix

1   Making Friends With the Qabalah   1
2   ABCs of the Qabalah and Their Role in Daily Life   9
3   Introducing the Qabalistic Tree of Life   55
4   A Guided Tour of the Qabalistic Tree of Life   64
5   The Qabalah and Other Spiritual Systems   109
6   Further Study and Meditation   138

    Resource Guide   146

ACKNOWLEDGEMENTS

My deepest appreciation to Andi, Angela, Anith, Ann, Annette, Annie, Bill, Bonni, Bonnie, Brinda, Christie, Cynthia, David, Deanne, Dona, Donna, Fran, Gayle, Helen, Jackie, Jan, Janel, Jennifer, Jenny, John, Jonah, Joseph, Joyce, Kelly, Kieran, Kurt, Laurie, Linda, Lisa, Louise, Mare, Melanie, Michele, Mona, Patti, Paul, Randy, Roberta, Sharon, Susan, Teresa and Trevor.

Extra special thanks to Terry Donaldson, John Gilbert, Joseph Nolen and my dearest, Bernard.

'TO RECEIVE'

The word Qabalah is translated from the Hebrew both to mean 'to receive' and 'from mouth to ear'. This suggests that the Qabalah is sent from on high to those who are open to receiving its teachings and is then passed on to others 'who have the ears to hear'. In the pages ahead, you will be presented with material that offers you the opportunity to understand yourself and the world around you from the Qabalistic point of view.

While reading, please remember that the Qabalah is known as the 'pathless path'. Instead of providing an exact formula for living, the Qabalah and its symbolic representation, the Tree of Life, offer guidelines for living. These guidelines are presented in the form of universal and natural laws, principles and truths which explain how we and the universe operate. This information may also serve as a personal adviser that assists you to find and follow your particular spiritual path. Simply, the study of the Qabalah is not about searching for the way or adopting another's way, but finding and following your way through life to higher consciousness.

It is now time for you to sit back, relax and ready yourself 'to receive' and, as my dear Jewish grandmother Sadie so often said, 'Enjoy, my sweet!'

With respect and love,

Amber Jayanti

MAKING FRIENDS
WITH THE QABALAH

QABALAH, 'THE YOGA OF THE WEST'

Yoga is an ancient spiritual discipline that is meant to bring health, harmony, inner peace and higher consciousness to those who practise it. The word 'yoga' means a link or connection, and its habitual performance helps one to become aware of the link or connection between physical and spiritual existence. In the early part of the twentieth century, the mystical visionary and Qabalist, Dion Fortune, termed the Qabalah 'the Yoga of the West'.

Like the Hindu yogic and Buddhist traditions, the Qabalah is ancient, dating from at least two centuries before the birth of Christ. Although suppressed and discredited by both the Christian and Jewish clergy due to fear and a lack of understanding, Qabalistic practices have been used by mystics throughout the ages. During times of religious persecution, such as the Spanish Inquisition, Qabalists among others were tortured and brutally murdered when their non-traditional beliefs were discovered. Similar to many other sources of truth, the Qabalah has also been disregarded as a meaningful body of spiritual wisdom.

There is a Qabalistic legend about Jesus and the rabbis of Jerusalem. After hearing Jesus speak at the great temple when he was twelve years of age, the rabbis recognized that he was a mystic and advised him to join the Essenes, the mystically oriented community located at the Dead Sea.[1] It is for this reason that many believe Rabbi Yeheshua ben Joseph (Jesus son of Joseph) or Jesus of Nazareth, was a Qabalist. This also explains why, in the Qabalistic system of spiritual mastery called 'Grades', the Grade associated with a very advanced level of spiritual devotion and ability is modelled after the Christ Consciousness. Study of the Qabalah and its symbolic representation, the Tree of Life, is further allied with Hindu yogic and Buddhist ideas in that the practical application of its principles assists us to live healthier and more well-balanced lives. These principles function like tools to raise our level of awareness and, by doing so, help to improve our attitudes toward our daily work and responsibilities, as well as ease the suffering in the world around us – human, animal and environmental. The Qabalah is also a means through which one may become acquainted with the one divine Self or *Yekhidah*, as it is called in Hebrew, that exists within each one of us. (A capital S on the word Self indicates the sacred Self within each of us.)

WHAT'S IN A WORD?

Qabalah is a unique word that has several different spellings, each with a different meaning. The following are the most widely recognized definitions.

KABBALAH

Kabbalah is a body of mystical Jewish doctrines about the nature of divinity and the vital role that humanity plays in the divine plan.

Kabbalah is only one of several words used over the last two thousand years to designate the mystical Jewish movement, its teachings and followers. The earliest form of Kabbalah is linked to the works of Rabbi Schimeon ben Yochai who lived in Palestine or ancient Israel about 200 BC. As mentioned, it is also attributed to the Essenes, an ascetic Jewish sect that existed in Palestine from the second century BC to the third century AD.

The term 'Kabbalah' developed into the most commonly used term for Jewish mysticism during the Middle Ages. Many Jews, because of their religion, were expelled from Spain in 1492 and emigrated to Safed in Palestine. As a means of coming to terms with the terrible pain and humiliation of exile, these people developed passionate spiritual practices which were aimed at bringing the spirit of the Most High[2] to the earth. Unlike the earlier forms of Kabbalistic practice, which were limited to a learned and select few, this later form of Kabbalah was available to and could be practised by the masses. Out of this powerful mystical resurgence came movements such as the Lurianic school of Kabbalah, which is still taught and followed.

It is important to mention that Kabbalah has been influenced by other traditions. The fourteenth-century Spanish scholar and mystic, Abraham Abulafia of Saragossa, returned from his travels in North Africa and the Middle East with certain Hindu yogic techniques of sitting, breathing and rhythmic prayer that he and his disciples introduced into Kabbalistic rituals. These continue to be performed today.

More than Hinduism influenced Kabbalistic practice. Isaac the Blind, the thirteenth-century scholar from Provence, France, studied not only Jewish and early Greek and Christian mysticism, but writings by the mysterious Sufi brotherhood, the Brethren of Sincerity, or Ismailis, at Basra, Persia. These works, particularly *The Epistles of the Sincere Brethren*, greatly influenced the secret meanings of numbers, words, names and letters studied by ancient and modern Kabbalists alike. It is notable that, much in the way that traditional Judaism and Christianity

discredited their mystical movements, conservative Muslims did likewise to the Sufis.

THREE MAJOR WORKS

The ancient Jews produced three major works: The Old Testament, which contains the main body of Jewish law and tradition; the Talmud, the collection of scholarly commentaries on the Old Testament; and the Kabbalah, the mystical interpretation of both the Old Testament and Talmud.

The two major works of the modern Kabbalah are the Book of Splendour or *Zohar* and the Book of Creation or *Sefer Yetzirah*. The Book of Splendour, written by Rabbi Moses de Leon in the early thirteenth century, is believed to be a collection of the writings of Rabbi Schimeon ben Yochai dating from around 200 BC. Although once thought to be the work of the ancient Jewish Patriarch Abraham, The Book of Creation appears to have been written about AD 600 by an unknown mystic. Although some disagree, Chasidism, the works of the eighteenth-century Eastern-European Jewish ecstatic known as the *Ba'al Shem Tov* (Master of the Good Name), are part of the modern Kabbalah.

CABALA

Cabala is the spelling used when discussing the spread of the Jewish mystical tradition, Kabbalah, and its symbols into mystical Muslim and Christian circles. This movement originated in Persia in the tenth and eleventh centuries and appeared in southern France and Spain in the twelfth and thirteenth centuries. Interest extended into the Italian Renaissance, and Cabala was among the material studied at the Medicean Academy. It is quite likely that the catalyst for the formation of the Cabalists was a compelling interest in the early life and religious training of Jesus.

Although Cabala peaked during the Renaissance, attraction to it continued long afterwards. Those interested included

Meister Eckhart, Raymond Lully, Pico della Mirandola, Lorenzo de Medici, Cornelius Agrippa, Guilliam Postel (who translated the Book of Splendour and Book of Formation into Latin), Jacob Boehme and William Blake.

QABALAH

Qabalah is the mid-nineteenth century spelling that refers to a body of esoteric and practical knowledge that blends Judeo-Christian mysticism (the Kabbalah and Cabala) with the teachings of other disciplines – most notably the Hermetic arts and sciences such as tarot, astrology, alchemy, numerology and sacred geometry. From this commingling came the Qabalah, also known as the Universal Qabalah, which, by its name, states that it is *not* limited to or associated with any particular religious denomination. Because I have been trained in this type of Qabalah, I use this spelling.

THE UNIVERSAL QABALAH

The Universal Qabalah also includes material from Hindu yoga, Buddhism, Sufism, the ancient Hellenistic, Pythagorean, Gnostic and Neo-Platonic mystery schools, as well as from the more modern Masonic, Rosicrucian, Theosophical and Golden Dawn orders. Universal Qabalah is an inclusive system of beliefs and teachings that serves as a bridge between the inner traditions of the East and West, because it emphasizes the principles that these have in common. The study and practical application of both the Qabalah and its symbolic representation, the Tree of Life, have proven to enhance and add to the teachings of all spiritual belief systems.

Because the Qabalistic tradition teaches a 'natural religion', honouring a generic God who may be approached without the traditional sacraments or faith in Christ, it has often been discredited. Simply, Qabalah's universalism offends any group

that expresses exclusive claims about *the* way to know God and achieve salvation.

The Qabalists assigned the twenty-two letters of the Hebrew Alphabet to the Tarot's twenty-two Major Arcana cards and thereby to the twenty-two pathways on the Tree of Life (Figure 1). Qabalists believe that the Tarot is both a pictorial representation and a synthesis of the spiritual disciplines, mystery school traditions and orders mentioned above.

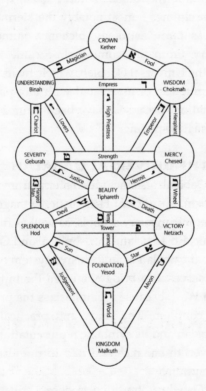

Figure 1 The twenty-two letters of the Hebrew alphabet and twenty-two cards of the Tarot's Major Arcana assigned to the Qabalistic Tree of Life.

Some people have found that conventional religion does not meet many of their deeper spiritual needs, nor answer some of their most pressing questions about their role in life. Because of this, they are now turning to the esoteric teachings of their Judeo-Christian roots for guidance and direction. The term 'esoteric' refers to the inner, secret or mystical beliefs, teachings and practices of a religious tradition. Because these tend to be more difficult for the average person to understand and responsibly apply than orthodox or exoteric religion, such teachings have been kept out of the reach of the general public. Like the tale of the sorcerer's apprentice, every esoteric school has its story of immature and impatient students who abuse and misuse their training and end up harming both themselves and others.

There is an old saying 'when the student is ready the teacher appears'. Since an increasing number of individuals have begun to seek this information, the esoteric traditions are now more open and accessible to society at large. Qabalah and Tree of Life study is gaining increasing attention and interest. Furthermore, the teachings of the inclusive Universal Qabalah are especially intriguing because we are living in a more global community in which both interfaith and interracial relationships are increasing, causing old prejudices to slowly fade away.

PRINCIPLES OF THE QABALAH

A principle is defined as a basic truth, law or theory and this book aims to introduce you to the ABCs of the Qabalah and the variety of ways in which it may be used. You will find out about the Qabalistic outlook on life and what it means to be a responsible and self-regulating member of the human family. You will be presented with the answers to questions such as: Is God a male or female? What is the Qabalistic Tree of Life? Do Qabalists believe in reincarnation? Must I love everyone? Are Qabalists vegetarians? What are the Qabalistic views on sex, abortion, divorce and homosexuality? And how do Qabalists relate to the environmental movement?

You will also be taken on a guided tour of the Tree of Life and shown its place in numerous cultures. You will receive an overview of its connections with the human body and chakra system, the tarot, astrology, sacred geometry, numerology and angelology. Finally, you will have the chance to consider various types of Qabalistic meditation and some options for further study.

By reading this book, you are giving yourself both a tool and the opportunity to learn the basic principles of the Qabalah and discover whether you wish to continue to explore this ancient yet ageless system.

NOTES

1 The Essenes are the group believed to be responsible for the creation of the world-famous Dead Sea Scrolls.
2 The Most High is a genderless name used by Qabalists to signify the Godhead which includes both God and Goddess.

ABCS OF THE QABALAH AND THEIR ROLE IN DAILY LIFE

TWELVE BASIC QABALISTIC PRINCIPLES

The following basic Qabalistic principles may be found within many, if not all, of the world's great religio-spiritual traditions.

One   All comes from the One Universal Mind. The entire physical universe is the Most High 'coming into being'. Qabalists believe that there is holy universal substance from which the human, animal, vegetable and mineral kingdoms originate and live and without which they would not exist.

Two   Physical reality is spiritual reality thought into form. The process of creation is actually the transformation of the imperceptible superphysical into the perceptible physical by the One Universal Mind. This means that what is in the godhead is also in us. The Most High is everywhere. This idea is often expressed by the ancient Hermetic axiom, 'As above, so below; as below, so above.'

Three   Knowledge of the Most High. Human beings may not only think about the divine, we may experience or 'know' the divine through the power of our intuition, or inner teacher.

Four We are limited and unlimited beings. We humans possess two natures: a personal or finite and limited self and an impersonal or infinite and unlimited Self. It is possible for each human to become completely identified with his/her infinite or eternal Self.

Five Unity with Self. The goal of each human life is for each of us, in our own way and time, to identify with our infinite Self and by doing so, to become one with it.

Six Polarity. All of creation is made up of positive and negative poles which may also be termed maleness and femaleness. The difference between things which are diametrically opposed to one another such as light and darkness, hot and cold, North and South, is a matter of degree. Every set of opposites may be reconciled.

Seven Vibration. All of creation – from sub-atomic to atomic particles and molecules within each creature and thing, to the planets rotating in their orbits – moves and vibrates at a particular rate or frequency. The denser the form the slower the movement and lower the rate of vibration. The lighter the form the faster the movement and higher the rate of vibration.

Eight Rhythm. Everything has its rhythm, its time and season to grow, flourish, decay and die. Change is unavoidable and constant. Everything that flows out must eventually flow back in. What rises will also fall. When there is an action there will be some type of reaction. If there is movement in one direction, movement is bound to occur in the opposite direction.

This law of nature explains everything from the turn of the seasons, change of the tides, to birth and death. It also accounts for the rise and fall of governments, economic, social and political backlash as well as the return of certain colours, styles of furniture, hair and clothing.

Nine   Cause and Effect. Each cause or action has its effect or reaction. Nothing escapes cause and effect or the workings of karma.

While all occurrences fall under the law of karma, there are times when what happens to or around us is not so much a personal repercussion as it is an opportunity for us to step up and deal with a random or synchronistic set of circumstances. Whether this means administering the Heimlich manoeuvre to someone who is choking, putting oneself in danger by pulling someone from a rain-swollen river or rescuing a neighbour's pets from an oncoming tornado, our role is one of hearing the call and then answering it. Actions such as these offer us the chance to adjust or mitigate the workings of karma.

Ten   Free Will. The freedom to choose what we think, say and do plays a role in determining effects or karma.

Eleven   Responsibility. We must be willing to take personal responsibility for what results from the choices we make.

Twelve   All is Perfect. When observing life from the cosmic or spiritual point of view, every event takes place in the perfect way and time.

The following sections give examples of how these basic principles, and others, are interwoven into the Qabalistic way of life.

FROM THE ONE COMES THE MANY

From the astrophysical point of view, the Big Bang affirms the singularity or 'oneness' at the beginning of the universe. Qabalists believe that the entire world is the Most High's creation. The One Universal Mind produces the manyness of physical existence. This event may be compared to Aristotle's cause of all causes or Prime Mover, the self-stirred Existence that jump starts the universal life force into motion and the world into being.

MIND OVER MATTER

Whether it is the Universal Mind or godhead intending to create the manifest world, or a human mind intending to create a work of art, the process is identical. Set the intention to create, followed by the conscious attention to actually do so. Most ancient religions regarded each and every form of creativity to be divine in origin. This principle has been carried over in the use of modern language. For example, we speak of the creative 'inspiration' which brings new ideas to the world and shapes physical reality. Because the divine mind is so powerful, *anything* it thinks is, too! Qabalists believe that the world is made by mind, sustained by mind and destroyed by mind – whether it is the One great impersonal mind or one's own mind. Therefore, in the ordinary sense of reality, nothing exists at all; everything is made of mental substance. If you think you live in the world, think again. You live in your mind, which lives in the One Mind.

THE MOST HIGH IS EVERYWHERE AND IN EVERYTHING!

One of the primary Qabalistic principles is that the Most High is omnipresent – is everywhere and in everything. This means that all that exists is divine in essence and origin. An essential part of the Qabalist's spiritual practice is aimed at assimilating the fact that the earth and all of its inhabitants are manifestations of the one sacred spirit of life.

Because the entire physical universe originates or emanates from the same source and is in all, the same natural laws and principles apply to each and every particle of life, from the smallest to the largest. This concept helps to explain the Principle of Correspondence, 'As above, so below; as below, so above'. Over time and with maturity, the Qabalist becomes increasingly able to actually see, hear, feel and sense the holiness of the Most High everywhere – in all people, creatures, things, places and situations at all times. When we develop the ability to hold this point of view consistently we are 'enlight-ened,' or able to perceive the sacred light of the Most High within each and every physical form.

MUST I LOVE EVERYONE?

Many people misinterpret the principle that the divine is in all, by thinking that they *must* love everyone. They become both disappointed with themselves and disillusioned with the spiritual teachings that they are following when they are unable to do so. In reality, Qabalists are *not* expected to love every personality but to become able to respect and honour the holiness that exists at the core of each individual.

Developed Qabalists are able to look beyond the personality to the sacred Self that lives within the hearts of others. This ability translates into sensible behaviours such as not marrying or entering into a business partnership with some people, yet being able to sincerely wish those individuals well because they are, in essence, a child of the Most High. Enlightened individuals always remember that they have the one holy spirit in common with everyone.

The Qabalistic Principle of Polarity defines positive and negative as two poles of the same one thing, with countless degrees of difference between them.

The Old Testament's Book of Genesis 1:26 states 'And God said, "Let *us* make man in *our* image, after *our* likeness".'[1] Inaccurate translations of the Bible from its original texts turned God into a masculine figure. The original word for 'God' used in Genesis was *Yahweh Elohim*, which when translated from the ancient Hebrew, actually means *both* God the Father and Goddess the Mother.

Looking at the Tree of Life you can see that these two aspects of deity, named Wisdom and Understanding, Father God and Mother Goddess, respectively, originate from the One, or the Crown. It is this One that divides itself to create the male and female deities and the positive and negative polarities or forces. This phenomenon also illustrates that God is both male and female! Therefore, whether occurring on the universal or personal level, creation is the result of the coupling of this divine pair.

In summary: Everything originates from the One. The One creates the two poles. Each and every physical form contains some combination of these polarities. Although the physical world does fall into the categories of male and female, positive and negative forces, it is One force at its core.

ORIGINAL GODNESS

Qabalistic wisdom offers a simple, yet important change of perspective from that of more conventional belief systems. Instead of regarding ourselves to be innately sinful, we are the children of the Most High and are filled with Original Godness. This principle does not mean we are incapable of evil acts, it simply affirms our divine parentage. After all, the Most High contains both positive and negative polarities, or good and evil, and we may *choose* to behave like gods or demons.

Original Godness allows us to act as conscious *co-creators*, meaning that we have the same creative powers as the Most High. The Principle of Co-Creation indicates that we are aware that we work along *with* the divine and that the one divine will takes precedent over personal will.

FREE WILL AND NO BLAME

Being a co-creator also means that we have the power of Free Will. We may choose: 1) how we interpret what we think and feel; 2) whether or not to act upon our thoughts and feelings; 3) what is the best course of action to take should we decide to act; and 4) how to relate to what arises from our plan of action.

Along with the will to choose comes the opportunity for us to be responsible for what we decide. If things do not work out as planned, we do not blame others for our decisions and subsequent acts. We also have the option to learn from the effects or karmic feedback that comes from actions. It is no wonder that many a Christian and Hebrew elder has felt threatened by the Qabalah!

MORE ABOUT THE PRINCIPLE OF CO-CREATION

Qabalists do not believe that they create as the divine Creator/Creatrix, who is all-present, powerful, seeing and knowing, but as co-creators, who see and know only a part of the whole of scheme of things. This means that as co-creators we may get ideas, imagine the various ways in which these ideas may take form, plot out a course of action through which we might manifest the form we select, and do the physical work

needed to make our dreams into realities. However, the co-creator also knows that the *ultimate* manifestation of his/her goal depends upon whether or not there is a need and place in the world for what he/she is co-creating. Success further relies on the ways in which what we are doing are necessary for our spiritual growth.

TIMING AND NON-ATTACHMENT

The manifestation of our co-creations or creative endeavours also hinges upon timing. Simply, if what we wish to bring into the world is right for the time, it will be born. Whether its full worth is recognized, is an entirely different discussion! Also, co-creators do not get overly attached to a specific time in which they will manifest their goals. For example, it is one thing to complete a writing project by a given date, but quite another to meet the love of one's life by a particular day or time. Qabalistic co-creators are certain that they will have tangible results in 'divine time'. We do the best we are capable of, while at the same time we remain healthily detached from the end result. The Principle of Non-attachment, or acting without being overly attached to what results, is not only set forth in the Qabalah, but in the teachings of the Hindus, Buddhists and Sufis among others.

Here is an example of the preceding principles in action: I decide that I want the book you are now reading to become an international best-seller. Although I am consistently told how valuable the book is and do my best to promote my work, which includes praying for and visu-alizing its success, I must also let go of the outcome. I do this because I realize that success will only prevail *when* a great number of people become so interested in the subject and my particular approach that they buy the book, and if the experience of having a 'bestseller' is what my soul needs in order to grow closer to the Most High.

Qabalists believe that someone who has not experienced the fire of their passions and desires has not really overcome them. When in this state, they may at any moment flare up to set us and our world on fire.

One Qabalistic statement tells us, 'Life is like a string of desires, which through their fulfilment, one after the other, brings us to higher consciousness.' Unlike spiritual and religious traditions which strive to kill desire, Qabalistic philosophy tells us that our desires, like everything else, come from the One. Because our desires come from the One, they have the potential to teach us about our *true* nature and how things *really* work.

Take some time to think about something you desire, then think about another, and another. You will discover that any effort to satisfy our desires not only sets the Principle of Cause and Effect or karma in motion, it asks that we work with other Qabalistic principles as well. In this way, the act of satisfying our desires offers us the chance to learn and grow. It is no coincidence that on the Qabalistic Tree of Life the sphere most associated with human desire is called Victory.

EATING THE FORBIDDEN APPLE

Much in the way that Adam and Eve were filled with a burning desire to eat the forbidden apple, we get similarly overwhelmed with what we yearn for. Adam and Eve *had* to eat from the Tree of Knowledge and experience the consequences, effect or karmic feedback derived from fulfilling themselves, and so do we. This is one of the main ways in which we reach spiritual maturity. Therefore, the Qabalist's goal is not to be desireless, but to desire that what we discover over time and through trial and error is best for us. What our cravings shows us is whether we have learned from past actions or not – has our passion

turned into compassion – and whether we need to repeat a lesson or move on to a new one.

> This principle is seen in the story of Sue driving her new tangerine-coloured convertible. After having one minor accident and earning two speeding tickets, has Sue learned that her tendency to drive fast is both dangerous and costly? Or does she now need to move on to have a major accident or get another speeding ticket and lose her driver's licence?

DESTRUCTION, INSTRUCTION AND CONSTRUCTION

Finally, while it is true that our desires may activate the forces of destruction, they are potentially instructive and constructive.

> Jonathan, a man who regularly keeps his anger bottled up realizes that he needs to show his feelings. He does this by impulsively hurling his dinner plate filled with food across the room. After doing this, he finds that he must not only clean up the mess, but that he has both frightened his family and provided his children with a negative model regarding the expression of anger. This disastrous experience does hold the potential to be instructive and constructive. When Jonathan learns how to take hold of his childish urge and create a better way to vent his feelings, his destructive action becomes both instructive and constructive in nature.

SELF-REGULATION

One of the Qabalist's primary goals is to become self-regulating. Self-regulation calls up the Principles of Free Will and Discernment. Self-regulation means that we consciously *choose* how to behave in an ever-increasing number of situations. This behaviour is based upon the intent to do what is for the greater good of ourselves and others, plus the desire to live with clear conscience. It is developed by way of the feedback that we receive from our actions.

Self-regulation indicates that the Qabalist is aware that his/her personality is always under the direction of his/her higher or spiritual Self. In other words, although it appears that we run our lives, our higher Self is the force that *really* runs us. It is for these reasons that self-regulation goes hand in hand with openness to receive guidance from our intuition as well as from other tried and true sources of inspiration.

Until we mature to the point where we are capable of figuring out and maintaining our own code for living, our family, culture, social and religious institutions provide these rules and regulations for us. An important part of our spiritual evolution involves learning how to *discern* between what these external forces ask of us and what is correct for us to ask of ourselves. Discernment further means being able to determine whether what we have been trained to do automatically is what we would still do if given the chance to consider our actions carefully.

LET YOUR CONSCIENCE BE YOUR GUIDE!

Qabalists believe that as we evolve spiritually, we become better able to listen to our conscience, the small quiet voice of truth within our heart of hearts, and let it guide us. In this way we learn how to live by what is morally and ethically correct.

While it is often necessary and helpful to be given behavioural guidelines, some of these are best adopted only *after* one has fully considered both the alternatives of not doing so and the consequences which might follow. In many situations, consideration includes a certain amount of experimentation that engenders

the Principles of Cause and Effect. Please bear in mind, though, that to experiment does not mean one throws *everything* that one knows to be right and wrong out the window!

DAVID'S DILEMMA

For as long as he could remember, David's family repeatedly told him that it was a sin for him to date or marry a woman outside of his own race or religion. Along with this value, he was also instilled with the knowledge that, should he marry outside of his race or faith, he would be mourned as dead.

When David left home to go to college he became acquainted with young women from many different backgrounds and found several to be very attractive. This left him with the dilemma of deciding whether going against his family's values was essential to *his* moral integrity. One day, he phoned to tell me that he felt in his heart of hearts that he needed to experiment. It was only after dating and experiencing these women as people, rather than as a particular skin colour or religion, that he became able to decide whether adopting his family's code of behaviour was right for him.

'TRY AND SEE'

This is the way in which Qabalists determine whether or not to make certain moral and ethical values their own. A certain amount of 'try and see' which leads to self-knowledge is healthy, as it helps us to decide whether or not to adopt attitudes and behaviours which are different from those dictated by our family, peers, society and so forth. In essence, it is by being aware that we have chosen one specific course of action over another that we: 1) become able to evaluate what results from our decisions; 2) determine if we wish to incorporate a value into our code of behaviour; 3) figure out how to assume responsibility for our decision; and 4) get to know ourselves and by doing so, allow our conscience to guide us.

EMOTIONAL PAIN AND SUFFERING

The physical world and our bodies give us the opportunity for a unique type of spiritual growth. From the Qabalistic point of view, everything that happens to us is part of our spiritual development, and as such is regarded as an occasion to increase self-awareness. We accomplish this by training ourselves to see life's joys and pains, from both the physical and spiritual points of view. Awareness of Self also develops from the process of figuring out how *best* to handle what life presents us with. This means doing today what has a good chance of continuing to be right tomorrow.

A friend hung a sign on her kitchen wall which said, 'When life gives you lemons, make lemonade.' Pain and suffering are a call to pay attention to and alleviate what is occurring, yet at the same time to remember that, as human beings with limited perception, we may not always see the whole picture. Because of this, we may fail to understand the *exact* reason for our distress. In such instances understanding comes second to facing and doing what we can to change our situation for the better.

SELF-CORRECTION AND TRANSFORMATION

Pain, unhappiness and dis-ease offer us the feedback that we may have violated some natural or universal law. In some instances pain and suffering ask that we take a closer look at what we think and feel, as well as how we treat ourselves and others. Honest self-reflection offers us the opportunity to correct or alter our attitudes and actions. Pain and suffering also serve as potent inspirations to gain the skills and abilities, and in some instances the medicines, needed to help us relieve our

misery and by doing so transform us into better-adjusted and happier people. It is important to recognize that for many, dealing with such difficulties is the catalyst for spiritual awakening.

> A young woman firmly believes that all relationships are painful. Eventually – this might take years – she will be driven by her misery to find out how to *stop* her pain and suffering. Whether she is able to discover a specific *cause* for it or not, she will seek to change its *effect* upon her. Simply, she becomes able to take a certain amount of personal responsibility for her state and desires to learn how she might *regulate* her attitudes and behaviours so that they will no longer cause her heartbreak. By adjusting or altering and correcting her thoughts and actions, she starts to see herself and the world differently and experiences her spirit awakening.

MUST WE SUFFER TO GROW?

It is quite common to get the erroneous idea that unless we are in pain and are suffering, we are not growing. Pain and suffering, particularly at the onset of our spiritual journey, may function as a potent tool for our development. They are sometimes the only way we become aware of the true nature of our difficulties, but such experiences are not always necessary for continued progress. In other words, as we become increasingly tuned in and self-aware, we begin to notice *and* pay attention to the warnings that we previously missed or disregarded. Foresight and insight help us to adjust our behaviour so that we may possibly prevent tragedies from taking place.

WHAT IS ONE'S BEST EFFORT?

Another principle of the Qabalah deals with understanding what is one's *best* effort. Essentially, whatever an individual is *presently* able to do is, in fact, considered to be their best effort. This brings us face to face with another Qabalistic concept: from the universal point of view, we are *always* doing the very best we can do, no matter how much we might think otherwise. In other words, our having the knowledge of how to behave better does not necessarily mean that we *consistently* do so.

TWO GREAT CHALLENGES

We must meet two great challenges on the road to achieving our best effort and spiritual progress. The first occurs in situations when we would like to act differently, but because we are tired, upset or stressed, we resort to old habit patterns. The second happens when we act in newer and better ways, yet we find ourselves dealing with upsetting feelings that contradict what we have done, that manage to sneak up on us automatically.

Both these occurrences are *normal*. However, if we get into the habit of acknowledging and witnessing what is taking place, rather than becoming overly involved and hard on ourselves, such experiences have less impact.

ANGER

Whether or not we allow it to show, we all get angry. Anger is a secondary response to hurt, pain, fear and/or the inability to control one's life or others' actions. The lasting presence of this emotion tell us that something in our lives, or our view of life, may be out of balance. Part of the Qabalists' development is about learning how to come to terms with this and other emotions, and then redirecting our energies to work for, rather than against, us.

Life is full of situations in which anger is absolutely appropriate. The key, however, is discovering ways in which to use anger *productively* and *constructively*. To use it in this way means that, in most circumstances, we are able to exert power over our actions and feelings, and *not* over others. (Of course, there are certain instances when we are obliged to step in and forcefully stop others from harming themselves, us or another individual.)

THE PRINCIPLE OF SUBLIMATION

Because anger, like other powerful emotions, has a way of reappearing until it is handled, it may not be stuffed or stifled. Yet it may be redirected to help and not harm. Anger is sometimes the only way through which we can make changes in ourselves and initiate changes in the world. We get so furious that we decide, for example, 'I am going to do everything in my power to stop the mistreatment of homeless people.' The process of taking a potentially destructive impulse and redirecting it towards a more constructive end illustrates the Qabalistic Principle of Sublimation. Although many religio-spiritual systems teach that expressing, or even feeling, anger or other negative feelings goes against their teachings, Qabalists hold to a very different idea. We are taught that when the expression of anger is driven by our desire to change things for the better, it is a compassionate gesture towards both ourselves and others.

FEAR

The Qabalistic tradition also recognizes the important role that fear plays in our lives. We believe that fear is both a helpful and harmful emotion. When we knowingly act without conscience, it is *healthy* to be afraid of the consequences. But when we are put in the position of needing to learn something such as a new task at work, fear may prove to be *unhealthy*.

Like anger, fear may be turned to our advantage. It can potentially move us to do what is necessary, but is not always easy. Fear may be thought of as an alarm which warns us of impending danger. Fear might immobilize us in some instances, while in others it forces us to flee. Qabalists view fear as a signal to wake up. Fear may act as the impetus for change when we become aware of the consequences of failing to do so. For example, the fear of disaster has the potential to make a person want to cease drinking and driving.

Qabalists believe that it is essential to *feel* and *face* our fears, rather than blocking them out and pretending that we are not feeling as we do. Honest confrontation can potentially enable us to act upon what is scaring us in ways that will help us to handle and overcome what is causing us to be upset.

THE PRINCIPLE OF EVIL: THE DEVIL AND DIVINITY

It is no coincidence that the words 'devil' and 'divinity' originate from the same root, the Indo-European Devi, meaning Goddess, or Deva meaning God. The Qabalistic Principle of Polarity reminds us that evil and its opposite, good, are varying degrees of the same thing. Another basic principle of the Qabalah teaches that all things and experiences contain and are set in motion by the Most High. Instead of pitting evil and/or the Devil against good and/or God, Qabalists reason that if the Most High creates good and evil, we were meant to have both of these qualities. Qabalists believe that whatever life presents us with, including evil, plays a role in our spiritual unfoldment.

The idea of evil, the demonic or dark side of the Most High, exists in most belief systems. Evil is both the shadow or dark

side of the Most High and of us. When the godhead is portrayed without negative qualities, it makes it nearly impossible to accept the presence of these traits within ourselves. Qabalists see the workings of evil to be another method the Most High uses to draw us closer and make us whole. This is because the consequences of our evil or weak acts eventually make us turn to the Most High and universal truth and law for help. Righting the world's wrongs begins with our having the awareness and courage to face and handle our weaknesses. Doing so enables us to accept who we are in totality. It also confirms the concept that when we hold in and do not deal with our negative feelings they eventually surface in the form of evil acts or harmful consequences such as depression, a migraine headache, or heart attack.

EVIL AND THE TREE OF LIFE

On the Qabalistic Tree of Life, the concept of evil is explained by the workings of Severity, the fifth sphere. Severity is known as the left hand of the Most High, while the right hand is the opposite sphere, Mercy. While Severity does provide a necessary balance to Mercy, evil is seen as the unbalanced state of acting without Mercy or loving kindness. Behaviours of this sort stem from the intent and compulsion to cause harm and thereby lack the desire to mercifully assist or heal a situation. As long as our will to act in ways that are harsh or severe includes a measure of loving kindness, it is positive and beneficial. However, if a pain-provoking act lacks this essential ingredient, it becomes unnecessarily destructive and consequently evil.

Qabalists believe that evil exists. Yet, instead of teaching that people are innately sinful or possessed by the Devil, we believe that there are no evil people, only evil or unloving *acts*. The divine acts with loving intent. Yet, because we humans have not fully developed our ability to act as gods, evil occurs when our shortcomings get the best of us and we act without conscience. We perform actions of this sort with little or no thought about the consequences, but solely for the emotional release and personal satisfaction that acts like 'getting even' give us. We must be aware that when we purposefully hurt others, we hurt ourselves as well.

Although it is not always easy to stop and think about what motivates us to do harm, it is extremely beneficial to evaluate what is driving us, rather than acting purely from impulse or instinct.

COOLING OFF

I have learned through the results that have come from my taking action when I am overwhelmed with hurt, anger, fear and so on, that it is best to allow my feelings to subside rather than responding in a way that puts my impassioned needs first at *any* cost. Cooling off allows us to take a more objective look at our difficulties. In this state we are better able to consider how to remedy and heal a difficult situation, rather than continue it by causing further injury. Waiting a while before we act also permits us to think about how we might add the intent of doing what we believe to be most beneficial in the long run. Please do not misunderstand. This does not mean 'turning the other cheek'. It means doing what must be done, yet with the aim of doing what is for the greatest benefit of *all* concerned. This simply may come down to asking ourselves, 'Do I intend to heal and help rather than hurt and harm?'

REPENTANCE AND JUSTICE

People recognize and repent for their malevolent acts when *they* are ready to do so, not when others would like them to do so. Unless someone is genuinely ready or mature enough to change

his/her behaviour, the words or actions of others will not force this to happen. If you doubt this principle, just think about all the people in jails and prisons and the large number of repeat offenders. This fact can prove very difficult for the injured or the friends and relatives of those injured to swallow.

When another is unable to immediately right their wrongs or we do not know who did what, the harmed may benefit from trusting in the Principle of Cause and Effect. Although a victim or his/her loved ones may never see the effect or law of karma meted out, it will in time take place. Therefore, the best we can best do is to heal our hurts and trust in two Qabalistic concepts: 1) from the universal point of view, every event takes place in the perfect way; and 2) justice, like many other things, is always served in divine time.

OPPORTUNITIES

At this juncture it may prove valuable to recall that while all occurrences are included under the law of karma, there are instances when what transpires is not so much a direct repercussion as the result of random violence or synchronistic circumstances. These events may be seen as opportunities for victims and those close to them to move up the evolutionary scale by their taking an out-of-the-ordinary course of action.

This concept may be seen in these examples. An organization devoted to finding missing children was founded by the family of a young child who was kidnapped by a stranger while playing in his own home. A woman was physically forced to complete a very painful and highly invasive medical procedure after she told the physician to stop it. After several months of suffering she realized that she could not undo what was done to her, but she might be able to prevent it from being done to someone else. She did this by speaking at an open public forum sponsored by the Commission for the Prevention of Violence Against Women in the city in which she lives.

FATHER, MOTHER, LOVER AND FRIEND

Qabalists are mystics and to the mystic, the Most High is all and in all. Accounts of mystics throughout the ages state that, when observing the loving devotion with which these people relate to other people and creatures, one believes that person to be engaged in holy communion. Yet *before* feeling this type of love towards the physical world, the mystic usually falls in love with the spiritual world – God is love, lover and beloved. Much as one person develops a close relationship with another, the mystic develops a close personal relationship with the divine. This means that the mystic not only relates to the Most High as the perfect parent, the love of one's life, or dearest friend, but relies upon the Most High in much the same way. In such ways, the mystic then becomes aware of the divine presence enthroned in physical reality.

Jesus lovingly referred to the Most High as his father in heaven. The Hindu saint Mirabai sung about her love of Lord Krishna from dawn to dawn. Christian mystic and poet Mechthild of Magdenbury wrote of her union with God in such exquisite terms that readers are deeply moved by the passionate nature of her words and use of erotic symbolism. Gertrud the Great is said to have had enthralling talks with Jesus and Mary in dreamlike states. The Hindu master Sri Ramakrishna related to the Divine Mother as if she were a flesh-and-blood person. The Jewish ecstatic the Ba'al Shem Tov was so 'filled with God' that those in his congregation could actually sense the divine

among them. The Sufi saint Ibn al-Arabi lifted the spirits of those around him by preaching the fact that all are God's children.

Mystical consciousness occurs within the Qabalistic Tree of Life's Moral or Conscious Triad of Mercy, Severity and Beauty.

EQUILIBRIUM IS THE BASIS OF THE GREAT WORK!

Another principle of the Qabalah emphasizes the importance of equilibrium or inner stillness in the Great Work – centring on the one Supreme Self at all times. More precisely, the Great Work is the gradual process of integrating our spiritual beliefs and philosophy into our daily lives and, by doing so, living a more fulfilling life and achieving spiritual unity. It is actually our wish to succeed in life that brings us into contact with the Principle of Equilibrium. The Qabalistic Tree of Life illustrates this principle by way of its three pillars: Mercy, Severity and Equilibrium. All the great esoteric traditions teach their followers methods through which they may achieve Self-centred inner stillness. Whether it is Hatha Yoga exercises, Zen or Tibetan Buddhist meditation, or visualizing oneself as the Qabalistic Tree of Life, the goal is the same.

Here is an example of the Principle of Equilibrium in action. As I listened to a friend going on and on about her awful boss, I began feeling very impatient with her extremely negative attitude. Instead of cutting the conversation short and running away, I reached for equilibrium in the form of the Principle of Polarity and Law of Neutralization. The principle reminded me to look at *both* sides of the picture before I acted. After taking a few deep breaths to help centre myself, I soon recalled that this friend is not only an excessive talker and complainer, but she is also someone who is an excellent listener, and accepting of others. This shifted my mind into a more balanced place, which neutralized my internal judgements and discomfort, and helped me to regain my patience and attentiveness.

CENTRED IN SELF

Each and every physical body is always in the process of changing or rebalancing itself. Whether it is a biological change such as our blood sugar rising after we have eaten, our feelings shifting from anger to compassion after we more fully understand a situation, or flying in our dreams, we are *always* in the midst of some type of physical, mental and emotional adjustment. Although temporary, being equilibrated, balanced, or centred in Self is desirable because it enables us to think more clearly, act more responsibly and thereby live more successfully. It also helps us to feel less regret about what we say and do.

In some instances balance is purely a physiological process, while in others, it depends upon our ability to recognize that our perception is off and then correct it. In this sense, equilibrium may be seen as a kind of self-correction. Just as a rubber band rebounds when it is stretched in one direction, we tend to move in the opposite direction in order to equilibrate ourselves and regain our centre.

SHIFTING INTO NEUTRAL

As you can see, equilibrium requires the neutralization of two opposing or polarized forces, such as good and bad. Although equilibrium has many different forms and levels, it is always the result of finding a stable point between alternating and conflicting forces. For instance, how often do we think that something is absolutely wonderful and have it turn out to be absolutely awful. Or we believe a situation is completely terrible, then suddenly realize that we can gain something of great value from our experience. This is a form of neutralization. For these reasons many Qabalists subscribe to the Principle of Isness; that is, when we are equilibrated, life is neither all good nor all bad. 'It just *is*.' In this state, acting influences are cancelled by others, resulting in mental and emotional stability and a balanced or non-dualistic system.

FEELING IT ALL

Isness does not mean that Qabalists do not feel joy or sorrow. Much to the contrary. Qabalists are able to feel *all* of their feelings, yet they do not necessarily have to *act* upon each and every one of them. To help put things in perspective before taking action, one recalls that there usually is more to what life presents us with than what appears on the surface. This type of thinking can reduce or even eliminate overly emotional or intellectual reactions (stretching the rubber band too far in one direction) and bring us back to a more neutral and centred place.

While Qabalists believe that every action has the potential to teach us something and help us grow, being centred when acting helps us to experience less harsh effects from our actions. Mental, emotional and physical equilibrium bring spiritual equilibrium and spiritual equilibrium brings mental, emotional and physical equilibrium in return.

ISNESS

Qabalistic tradition teaches the Principle of Isness or non-duality. Because we live in a dualistic world and are socialized to think accordingly, the gradual change to non-dualistic thinking goes hand in hand with our evolution into higher levels of consciousness. The development of Isness, however, is usually preceded by our spending years (and most likely lifetimes) setting the concepts of good and bad, and right and wrong against one another. The Principle of Polarity reminds us that good and bad may be varying degrees of the same thing. On the Qabalistic Tree of Life, the Middle Pillar, which represents non-duality and neutrality, also represents the present moment. Isness means that we are here now, or we are fully attentive to whatever we are presently doing.

In the state of Isness, we are naturally open-minded and deeply interested in people, things and situations, yet we do not place value judgments on them. We are also the perfect witness, exemplifying what yogic teachings refer to as 'witness consciousness'. This is a type of behaviour where we are able to observe what is happening around us clearly, accurately and dispassionately. Because of this, we are more able to perceive universal and natural laws and principles operating in whatever is presented to us. Our behaviours are based upon the greater reality, represented on the Qabalistic Tree of Life by the spheres of the Crown, Wisdom and Understanding.

The adept, the title given to one who embodies the Principle of Isness in the Qabalistic tradition, does not have to strain or struggle. He or she has come to live in this way through the process of his/her spiritual evolution.

THE ADEPT

Qabalists recognize that most people react to what goes on in themselves and in the world based solely upon their personal experiences. Rather than categorizing people and events in this manner alone, the adept expertly uses both personal *and* impersonal standards by which to respond to life. In this way, the adept can take the position of Isness.

Isness is sometimes misinterpreted to mean that one is passive. Like anyone, there are situations in which the adept both

acts and does not act. In either event, the adept makes his/her decision from a Self-centred or equilibrated state. Here, he or she does not get caught up in black and white thinking but perceives the world in shades of grey or neutral. Doing this allows him/her to see the complete picture, rather than just its parts.

'IN THE WORLD, BUT NOT OF IT'

Qabalists also aim to embody the idea of 'being in the world, but not of it'. This principle means that we participate fully in daily life yet keep our spiritual point of view. This outlook enables us to refrain from becoming overly attached to the outcomes of situations and willing to do what is necessary, though at times difficult and unpleasant. In essence, we learn to listen, to give advice when asked, to act when conscience dictates, and to adhere to the concept that every person matures in his/her own way and time. Although we do our best to influence what goes on around us, we know in our heart of hearts that all events have their perfect place and outcome in the greater scheme of things and that the only thing we can ultimately control is our own attitudes and actions.

DEATH AND MOURNING

In the ancient Hindu *Bagavad Gita*, Lord Krishna tells his student Arjuna that 'The One who dwells within all living bodies remains forever indestructible'. Based upon this principle, Arjuna is instructed to never fear death or mourn. Krishna continues to state that while death is a certainty for all who are born, rebirth is as certain for the dead. For these reasons, one should not be afraid of what is inevitable.

Modern physics substantiates this ancient belief when it declares that matter is a temporary massing together of the pervasive energy that enlivens the electron. Nothing exists or is destroyed because all physical reality is energy which is continuously changing shape and form. Qabalists agree with both the ancient Hindu and modern scientific views. Although the physical body, which is matter, does decay and die, the soul, which is energy, is not lost. It converts itself into another form.

Qabalists believe that death *always* occurs in the way and time that is appropriate for the soul's development. (In some instances the living must have tremendous faith to accept this principle.) Also, we view death to be life's last initiation into the spiritual mysteries and as a great friend who brings relief from incurable pain and physical illness. Because life's most mysterious rite of passage is death, students of the Qabalistic mysteries are trained as early as possible to face this unavoidable fact of life. Life is considered to be a preparation for death, and the after-death experience is seen as a preparation for the lifetime ahead. Although Qabalists, like other esoteric practitioners, regard death as a physical, rather than a spiritual, fact, they do mourn. Mourning offers the living the chance to fully acknowledge the loss of the dead.

I was honestly relieved when my aged mother was freed from her severely ailing body. At the same time, I was deeply saddened that I would no longer be able to enjoy her interactions with my children, nor take her for a ride by the ocean on a Sunday afternoon and listen to her stories about life as a young woman in the early part of the twentieth century.

REINCARNATION

Most Qabalists have great faith in the idea of reincarnation. One reason reincarnation occurs is because the soul is unable to dissolve its physical attachments, such as to another person or life goal, at death, or it has resisted fulfilling its responsibilities. Attachments and aversions are what necessitate the soul's unrest and need to take on another lifetime in the physical world.

Each time a soul is reborn into a physical body, it has the opportunity to improve itself and the world by way of dealing with the conditions into which it has chosen to be born. These include: family relationships, culture, religion, geographical location, the social and political climate of the time, and of course one's physical characteristics and mental abilities.

Qabalists believe that a soul exists prior to the formation of the body in the world of spirit. The entrance of the soul into the body occurs because a soul has *both* an infinite or impersonal, and finite or personal nature. The soul unites with the body in order to better develop itself. The soul achieves perfection by playing particular parts in the world, which help it to become aware of its true nature and divine origin. After completing the work it has taken on, the soul returns to the world of spirit. It is further thought that when a soul has completely transmuted its finite nature, it ascends beyond the world of spirit to the godhead and oneness. In this state, any sense of oneself as a separate individual no longer exists, except in the memories of others on the physical plane.

SUICIDE

Every religio-spiritual group has its policies regarding suicide, and the Qabalistic tradition is no different. Due to the fact that today's Qabalistic school is a blend of ancient and modern thought, some of the earlier rules and regulations have been modified. Although we are not our body, the body does serve as the vehicle in and through which our soul and the one holy spirit lives and operates while we are on the earth plane. Because of this, killing the body is an *extremely* serious matter. Generally, suicide is a critical violation of both one's soul and one's spiritual integrity. Both the ancient and modern mystery schools concur that suicide is an unacceptable means of avoiding the potential for evolution inherent in sorrow and illness, or for that matter, *any* material world responsibility or difficulty.

There are, however, particular circumstances under which suicide is acceptable. In ancient times it was permitted to choose death over spiritual dishonour, as in the case of the spiritual warrior. An aspirant was allowed to take his/her own life rather than be subjected to torture which intended to force them to reveal the secrets of the mystery school to which one belonged. (This still goes on in certain parts of the world!) It was justifiable to sacrifice one's life in order to serve, preserve or pacify a deity. (I pray that this is not a present day event.) It remains acceptable, however, for one to give one's life in an effort to save another person from death or mortal danger – a type of sacrifice. Death was and still is an option if one becomes incapable of cognitive function, i.e. brain dead, and further spiritual development is no longer possible.

When one dies naturally, the soul detaches itself from the body. However, in suicide the body *forcibly* severs itself from the soul. Because this action goes against the laws of nature, it disorients the soul. We have all heard stories of the 'unquiet dead'. Undue death results in this terribly unsettled condition. One has destroyed one's body, yet has not lived out one's life cycle. It is for this reason that the unquiet dead are spiritually obligated to

remain in their astral or spirit bodies until the normal span of their life is finished.

> While living in great physical pain may not be tolerable for everyone, my own experiences of living in this state (due to a back injury) have proven to be valuable teachers. They have shown me that I am, without a doubt, much more than my physical body and that my mind has a great deal to do with what and how I am feeling. Because these periods have been relatively short – hours, days, weeks and months – I cannot judge what it would be like to live in such pain over a long period of time. In truth, suicide is another instance in which our enactment of the Principles of Free Will and Personal Responsibility are to be honoured.

HEAVEN OR HELL – IT'S UP TO YOU!

Qabalists believe the world is made by mind, sustained by mind and destroyed by mind. If you think you live in the world, think again. You live in your mind which lives in the Universal Mind. This principle has led many a Qabalist to believe that the concepts of heaven and hell are the result of how one thinks – one's belief system. In other words, if two people in the same situation can have two very different experiences of that event, might not this same principle be applied to our after-death experience? When we die, our physical body and personality are discarded and all that remains is our mind. The stepping away from the personality, the subjective or *non-objective* part of our being, takes place so that we may step into the soul-spirit state of impersonal awareness. In this spiritualized condition we become *objective* about both who we have been and how we have behaved during our time on earth. Simply, we come to be the judge of our actions. Whether we are able to accept what we

have done to be our best and desire to improve ourselves in the future is thought to determine to what degree we put ourselves into a mental heaven or hell.

TRASH BIN OR TEMPLE?

Many traditions teach that the physical body, its senses and desires for physical gratification, are a hindrance to one's quest for spiritual wisdom and understanding. Because the Qabalist believes that we are made in the image of the Most High, the physical body is considered holy, and it is treated with the respect and care holiness deserves. Consequently, the body is not considered to be an obstacle to spirituality but a precious instrument through which we receive spiritual awareness and fulfil our spiritual obligations.

The principle of respecting and caring for our body reiterates another Qabalistic principle: We are spiritual beings seeking to have a physical experience by way of which we deepen our knowledge of and intimacy with the one sacred spirit. The mystical poetry of Omar Khayya'm tell us:

> What you could not grasp here,
> How will you grasp it in a sphere,
> Where neither sense nor body adhere?

Each flesh-and-blood body is a temple in which the supreme consciousness lives and works. It is by way of the body, with its intellect and senses, that we may *actually* behold the Holy Spirit living in and around us. It is through the gradual refinement and clarification of how we sense physical reality that our ability to sense spiritual reality improves.

'GARBAGE IN – GARBAGE OUT'

An expression in computer jargon asserts, 'Garbage in – Garbage out.' In terms of our physical being this statement is interpreted to mean that when we treat our body like a trash bin, it becomes one. When we treat our body like a temple, it functions this way. Because the body is a means through which we experience the divine, Qabalists aim to lovingly regulate its appetites. Moderation and discipline, rather than a lackadaisical attitude and excess, help to keep our body fit and healthy, making it a better tool through which to fulfil our spiritual undertakings. Because the Middle Pillar of the Qabalistic Tree of Life is situated between the extremes of the Pillars of Mercy and Severity, it signifies both the Principles of Self-regulation and of Moderation.

DISEASE AND ILLNESS

Because we live and work in bodies of flesh, which are perishable, decay is inevitable. While it is true that disease and illness have the potential to function as potent teachers, we are also aware that some of these conditions may be avoided or lessened with proper care, insight and foresight.

For example, I have a genetic predisposition to adult diabetes, which may be brought on by poor diet and excessive stress. Many years ago this information prompted me to eat a well-balanced diet, including vitamin and mineral supplements, and develop a good programme of stress management. So far I have remained diabetes free.

A SPIRITUAL MISCONCEPTION

One spiritual misconception equates wellness with spirituality. This was abruptly brought to my attention when an acquaintance dropped her esteemed teacher of many years because he developed pancreatic cancer. She explained this by stating, 'At his level of spiritual development he should not become ill'.

An essential part of the Qabalists' spiritual growth and development comes from caring for the body both in sickness and in health. This means that, except in almost-unheard-of instances, physical illness and death are part of our spiritual journey. Qabalists understand that if and when our soul requires that we become ill in order to promote a certain kind of maturation, or to exit the physical body and world, it will take place.

FACING MENTAL ILLNESS

Because Qabalists recognize the value of having a sound mind, we are keenly aware of the influence biology asserts upon the mind and emotions. Biochemical insufficiencies or imbalances are known to result in a type of mental and emotional instability and fragility which severely limit our ability to think clearly to such a degree that our spiritual progress is made much more difficult. In the presence of certain neurobiological disorders such as schizophrenia, depression, mania, bipolar, obsessive-compulsive and attention deficit disorders, psychotropic medicines may stabilize neural activity when this is otherwise unlikely.

Unfortunately, some individuals remain in a state of ignorance or denial about the mental disarray incited by body chemistry – the difficulties brought on by such things as one's genetic predisposition and severe on-going stress. (It has been proven that psychological trauma can permanently impair neurological functioning.) There are also those who shun treatment because they fear the stigma of being diagnosed with a mental illness.

After thorough consideration, the Qabalist may opt to take a medication which balances his/her biology and thereby

improves brain function. In this way he/she may develop new cognitive maps which one may follow in place of psychoactive drugs when, and if, these are stopped. The developed Qabalist is able to face the fact that he/she is helped or obstructed by one of our greatest spiritual tools, the mind. When obstructions are present, we step out of our own way to sensibly seek out the means, be it prayer, meditation, study, therapy or medicine, through which we may regain mental clarity. I am acquainted with many Qabalists who regard the likes of Lithium, Prozac and Ritalin to be gifts from on high!

As in so many other instances, the Principles of Free Will, Cause and Effect, Rhythm, Personal Responsibility and Discrimination are once again brought into play.

VEGETABLES, MEAT, AND ALL YOU CAN EAT!

The Principles of Self-regulation and Moderation allow Qabalists to eat what benefits and maintains their health and vitality. Ideally, what a person decides to eat is derived from a basic understanding of what constitutes proper nutrition plus a keen awareness of one's bodily needs. In many instances, this decision is also a matter of one's religio-spiritual beliefs, medical needs – as in the case of cardio-vascular disease or diabetes – socio-economic status, and environmental and political viewpoints. These attitudes and ideas are illustrated in the following examples.

The Bible has instructed us not to eat fish that swim on the bottom of lakes, rivers or oceans, or animals with cloven hoofs. In order to eat meat one must be responsible for killing frightened and helpless animals. When one kills and/or eats an animal with reverence, one assimilates the energy and spirit of that creature. Grub worms are plentiful and therefore can be an important source of protein. Animal products are laden with harmful antibiotics, hormones, bacteria, toxins and chemicals. Certain essential minerals are only available in red meat.

The issue of who eats what is a wonderful opportunity to apply the Principles of Non-attachment and Non-judgement. These principles remind us to respect the fact that, while what another eats may not be right for our taste, it is right for them. I vividly recall a friend's father eating a mountain of french fried potatoes soon after suffering a heart attack. Some people need to follow their urges no matter what the consequences. At this juncture we might also consider how, at another point in our evolution, we may have done what they are now doing, or may even do so in the future.

THE BUDDHIST COW

These principles were permanently imprinted on me when, after practising strict vegetarianism for more than fifteen years, I was invited to dinner by the head lama of a Buddhist monastery in Nepal, only to be reverently served yak – the Nepalese equivalent to our cow. Eating this meal proved to be a valuable lesson, as it dispelled many of my stereotypes which erroneously tied diet to spirituality and ignored the matters of attitude and necessity. Recently someone told me that Adolf Hitler was supposedly a vegetarian – a contradiction to the vegetarians' presumed respect for living things!

SEX

Certain ideas about sex which were right at an earlier time in human society and personal development are no longer viable. Within the last fifty years, patterns of undue repression, guilt and inhibition have been dissolved so that we can move into a more evolved cycle of sexual expression. Please do not misunderstand:

Qabalistic principles regarding sex do *not* give people the freedom to do whatever they wish, whenever and with whomever they wish to do it. True freedom in any area of life, sexual or otherwise, requires that one has an elevated level of wisdom and understanding and behaves in accordance with one's awareness. It is our amended perception of what sex *really* is that makes misuse, degradation and shame less likely.

A BLESSED ACT

Qabalists use the term 'sex' differently from the majority of people. Like practitioners of the ancient form of yoga called Tantra, Qabalists view sex to be an extremely potent form of meditation which facilitates union with the Most High by way of union with one's partner. Because Qabalists believe that the physical body is the Holy Spirit in manifest form, sex is a blessed act which has the potential to bring about an ecstatic spiritual experience. Qabalists regard men and women to be equals or interdependent co-creators who empower and complement one another. Partners are seen as physical representations of the divine polarities of God and Goddess, the spheres of Wisdom and Understanding on the Qabalistic Tree of Life, respectively.[2]

Sex is a sacred meditation rite which takes various forms. Qabalistic sexual practices aim to raise one's spiritual energy, the Holy Spirit or Kundalini which resides at the base the spine, and by doing so to heal the damage done by separating sex from love. Because Qabalistic sex brings love back into the act of sex, it helps to create a truly ecstatic type of union, which begins, rather than ends, with consummation. In contrast to ordinary sexual practices where the goal of physical union is orgasm and procreation, sacred sex serves as a spiritual union that transmutes our physical energy into a more subtle form of creativity.

On the Qabalistic Tree of Life, this is seen as energy rising from Kingdom, the base of the spine, moving through Foundation, centre of the reproductive organs, and entering into Beauty, the heart centre. In time this force may also be directed up from the heart into the Crown of the Tree of Life or godhead, centre of pure spiritual consciousness.

UNCONDITIONAL LOVE IS AN ECSTATIC STATE

Sacred sex conjoins individuals with their spiritual Self. This kind of sex does not denigrate or exploit participants, but invokes and evokes unconditional love. Unconditional love is an ecstatic state, wherein one's heart is not only flung open to one's lover, but to everyone and everything! Union of this sort couples the positive and negative forces or the male and female polarities (the spheres of Wisdom and Understanding on the Qabalistic Tree of Life) within the individual into a type of mystical oneness. Participants achieve this by slowly and carefully raising the level of their spiritual energy by way of meditation, visualization, special breathing techniques and chanting.

Practice of sacred sex leads to a type of spiritual union not only during intercourse but afterwards as well, for it evokes the highest level of love possible between human beings and unifies partners on all seven planes of existence and in all seven bodies. These planes are represented on the Qabalistic Tree of Life as follows:

THE SEVEN PLANES OF EXISTENCE AND SEVEN BODIES AS RELATED TO THE TREE OF LIFE:

Spiritual Plane and Body:
The Crown

Causal Plane and Body:
Wisdom and Understanding

Higher Mental Plane and Body:
Mercy and Severity
Egoic[3] Plane and Body:
Beauty
Lower Mental Plane and Mental and Emotional Body:
Splendour and Victory
Astral Plane and Etheric Body:
Foundation
Physical Plane and Body:
Kingdom

To summarize: From the Qabalistic point of view sex is holy. The sexual relationship is not only about the coupling of two people, it is about each person's relationship and coupling with the one divine Self. Meditation techniques are used to help practitioners elevate their physical, mental, and emotional awareness in order to experience this state.

CELIBACY

Most of the world's great religious systems have monastic orders and in this way have encouraged asceticism and celibacy. Asceticism is the renunciation of personal belongings, thoughts and desires, one of which is celibacy or sexual abstinence. Because this is a short work I will only address celibacy, but these principles have been applied to asceticism.

Although celibacy is natural at a certain stage of evolution, as it helps the Qabalist to focus his/her attention and contain his/her energy, it is not something one *must* do. Qabalists teach that celibacy should be chosen, but not forced. A friend's story illustrates this idea. Ruth moved into a spiritual community in which unmarried people had to be celibate and married people could only have sexual relations once monthly. She soon became aware that community members were engaging in secretive sex and adulterous relationships. It was later learned that the celibate master was having sex with several of his young students. When celibacy is imposed, rather than chosen, failure is most likely.

Like the average person, the average Qabalist is unsuited for celibacy, and therefore it is generally not recommended. One cannot kill one's desires by suppression. They must die a natural death. Yet there are some instances in which celibacy is healthy and healing. It gives the Qabalist the opportunity to re-evaluate his/her attitude toward sex. There are other situations where celibacy is used to cover up an actual physical dysfunction, an unhealthy fear of sex and intimacy or in some cases homosexuality. When considering celibacy as an option, we must allow our conscience to be our guide.

HOMOSEXUALITY

We might consider that numerous sexual taboos against homosexuality began in the needs of the past, many of which related to issues of human survival – the mortality rate was considerably higher and the life span was shorter. Today these prohibitions make up part of the worn-out systems and philosophies which, besides spreading the teachings of the groups that originated them, spread hatred and intolerance.

The Qabalistic view of homosexuality is quite simple. Much as we respect and admire heterosexual relationships that are loving and do not demean or purposefully cause injury, we respect and admire homosexual relationships that do the same. Modern Qabalists regard homosexuality to be like other aspects of the human personality, an opportunity through which soul development may take place.

MARRIAGE: LOVE IS CONTAGIOUS

Like sex, marriage is a sacred rite. Qabalistic wedlock is an unconditionally loving, deeply intimate and fully committed relationship with another person that also functions to bring the human personality into a wedded state with the divine. This occurs because marriage is thought of as an alchemical process in which the interactions between partners serve to refine personal imperfections. As a result of these transmutations or changes, the relationship thrives and the relationship to one's higher Self becomes increasingly evident.

The difficulties which arise in marriage are believed to relate to each person's spiritual evolution and are dealt with accordingly. This means partners are appropriately available and helpful, yet realize that they often can do no more than to provide a safe and loving environment into which their mate may enter. Qabalistic marriage is additionally transformative in that partners focus on the essential divinity of one another, and by doing so, learn to focus on this quality within themselves as well as in the world around them.

Qabalistic marriage is not only about two individuals bringing their lives together, it is also the conjoining of each person with their higher Self, by way of their partner. This means that the conscious commitment or marriage contract affirms each partner's intention to access, integrate and thereby balance their male and female sides or polarities in order to live from their heart of hearts and be their true Self. A man's unconditional love of a woman transforms her into a vehicle for the divine feminine principle, much as a woman's unconditional love for a man transforms him into a vehicle for the divine masculine principle, Goddess and God, respectively.

Love is contagious! This type of relationship makes one a happier, healthier, more aware and well-balanced person. As partners become better at loving one another, they become better at loving themselves and eventually carry this love into *all* areas of their lives. Qabalistic marriage serves as a means through which universal wisdom, understanding and love actually flows out to other humans, creatures and things, and even into one's most ordinary activities.

SOUL MATES

Many people have spent a great deal of time, and in some instances money, searching for their 'soul mate' or 'perfect' other half, when in truth one would *not* be attracted to such a person even if they did meet. The reason for this lies in the principle that if one is not perfect themselves, one will tend not to *recognize* perfection in another. Simply, our soul mate is the person whom we are *presently* with. We gravitate to the relationships we do because they help us to become better acquainted with love, who we really are, and what we truly need to fulfil ourselves and know the divine.

DIVORCE QABALAH-STYLE

Because the principles involved in conscious decision-making carry over to the complex issue of divorce, Qabalistic divorce is a matter of trusting in one's ability to make a conscious and fully educated choice and then carry it out. To feel confident about doing this, the Qabalist searches his/her soul carefully *before* deciding whether divorce is the appropriate way to solve one's marital problems.

The Qabalist: 1) is clear about his/her *true* reasons for wanting a divorce; 2) considers the possible long-term results that breaking-up for such reasons might have upon one's life and children; 3) is willing to take *full* responsibility for his/her

decision to marry his/her partner, which includes sharing the responsibility for the divorce. In this mindset, liability is not placed upon one person, but both.

After exploring these areas, one is better equipped to listen to one's conscience or heart of hearts and make a decision that is intended to be for the greater good of all concerned. Remember that, while divorce is about making peace with our decision, it is also about how we treat ourselves and our spouse while going through the decision-making, divorce and/or reconciliation processes as well.

ABORTION – A MORTAL SIN?

Many groups teach that having an abortion is a mortal sin. Qabalists have a different point of view about this often 'too hot to handle' issue.

Here again, Qabalists favour conscious decision-making, as abortion is yet another arena wherein the Principle of Free Will – and all that goes with it – comes into play. For this reason, it becomes essential to carefully consider *why* one wishes to terminate or continue a pregnancy. Difficult as this might be, this journey may involve taking a look at the following types of question: If I were not able to conceive another child, would I have this one? I am barely able to support the children I now have. How am I going to care for another child without giving him/her even less than they now have? How would I feel about giving my baby up for adoption? Would I feel the same about having the type of adoption where I would still get to participate in my child's life? Before bringing our lives together my partner and I agreed that we did not want to have children. I changed my mind without telling him, and I am now pregnant. Which relationship is more important – the one with my partner or with the unborn child? I accidentally became pregnant at the

same time I got accepted to medical school. What might my future be like if I choose not to attend school at this time?

The Qabalist's decision about abortion is not a matter of blindly or fearfully following the dictates of others, but of believing in and honouring one's own intelligence and moral fibre.

SERVICE TO OTHERS

Service or charity to other human beings is essential. Offering humane treatment to others in the form of relief, support and comfort is considered to be service to the Most High in physical form. Qabalists feel morally bound to alleviate suffering when and where it is needed. Akin to many of the world's great traditions, we believe that when one person suffers, everyone suffers.

Charitable acts are seen as striking a balance between the principles of Mercy and Severity on the Tree of Life. When Mercy or generosity is unbalanced it may turn into an act of overindulgence. Severity, the force of loving correction, can check and rebalance this type of action, and the lack of generosity stemming from excessive Severity may be tempered by the loving kindness and compassion of Mercy. Even with the best of intentions, help given or withheld without conscious decision-making has harmed many a giver and receiver.

An effective way to decide how much help is appropriate is found by turning inward. Honest self-reflection aids us in discovering our true reasons for giving or holding back assistance. It also enables us to define our personal boundaries and limitations and to become aware of and accept the pros and cons of our potential actions.

HELP OR HINDRANCE?

As in so many other areas of the Qabalist's life, the Principles of Self-Regulation, Personal Responsibility and Non-attachment are highlighted. Qabalists become skilled at asking themselves questions such as: Am I doing this act for the recognition of others, or strictly for the satisfaction of giving? Would it be more appropriate and/or effective to give anonymously rather than to be known? Am I helping because I want this person to behave differently – like me more, divorce her abusive husband and marry me? Can I act because I know it is the right thing to do, but then let go of the outcome? Might giving actually be taking the course of least resistance? (Do I give my son money so that he will stop pestering me, rather taking the time to find out why he has again overspent his budget?) Is what I wish to give appropriate to what is needed? Could it be a more helpful gesture not to assist another and by doing so encourage that person to develop the strength and abilities necessary to help themselves?

Service to others also teaches the Principle of Self-Care First. The Qabalist is required to minister to his/her own basic needs prior to ministering to others. Therefore, one does not feed others when one's children are hungry. On the other hand, one will donate one's extra winter coat to charity before purchasing a new one.

KEEPERS OF THE GARDEN OF EDEN: QABALISTS AND THE ENVIRONMENT

Because the Earth and her creatures are also holy in essence and origin, loving care of the environment is as important to the Qabalist as the humane treatment of themselves and others. According to the Qabalistic interpretation of the Bible's Book of Genesis, Adam (or *all* the sons and daughters of the

Most High) was charged with the role of being a 'keeper' or caretaker of the Garden of Eden – a biblical name for the planet on which we live. Each one of us was created to fulfil our personal purpose, a part of which includes the compassionate treatment of the earth and all upon it. It can prove insightful to read the words of Genesis 1:24–28 with this in mind. Qabalists interpret the final verse, 'And God blessed them; and God said unto them [the humans]: "Be fruitful and multiply, and replenish the earth, and subdue it; and have dominion over the fish of the sea, and over the fowl of the air, and over every living thing that creepeth upon the earth" ', particularly the concept of 'dominion', to mean that human beings are spiritually obligated to exert a protective influence over the animal, vegetable and mineral realms. Humans are seen as the intermediaries between the heavenly and earthly worlds. As the creatures who were made in the image of the Most High and created last in the cosmic order, we were given the honour of caring for the Earth. Therefore, a part of each human's place in both the divine plan and natural order of things is to uphold the planet's well-being. This view pervades today's Qabalistic community wherein a considerable part of one's spiritual practice is aimed at assimilating the principle that the earth and all of its inhabitants are manifestations of the one sacred spirit of life.

NOTES

1 *The Holy Scriptures According to the Masoretic Text* (Philadelphia: The Jewish Publication Society of America, 1963) page 4.
2 While many of these practices are designed to unite male and female bodies and polarities, some may also be used by partners of the same sex.

3 In Qabalah the terms 'ego' and 'self-conscious awareness' are used interchangeably to mean the source of divine individuality which exists within every human being. It is also used to indicate the personality component that is conscious or aware of itself being a vehicle through which the Supreme Self expresses itself in the physical world.

INTRODUCING THE
QABALISTIC TREE OF LIFE

SHORTHAND FOR THE QABALAH

Because the Universal Qabalah encompasses the esoteric traditions of both West and East, you may find it easier to start with
its symbolic representation, the Qabalistic Tree of Life, which
presents its fundamental principles in pictorial form. Since
symbols are physical representations of non-physical truths,
laws and theories, the Tree of Life is a type of shorthand for this
mystical system. The next part of this book visually presents the
principles of the Qabalah via the Tree of Life.

To help you more fully understand the Qabalistic Tree of Life,
I will begin by explaining the many ways in which trees have
served humanity as maps of divine and human activities in the
form of oracles, healers, fertility, wisdom and immortality symbols, and the homes for ancestral spirits, gods and goddesses.
Trees have also been used to signify both the change of seasons
and ebb and flow of the life cycle.

TREES ACROSS TIME AND CULTURE

Some trees remain forever green while others bud, blossom,
bear fruit, shed their leaves and appear dead, yet come to life

again in another season. Because trees are seen to signify eternal life as well as the cycles of nature and human life, many groups have held them in high esteem since the beginning of human history.

From most ancient times, trees have been considered holy and dedicated to sacred use. The European Maypole, originally a symbol of fertility, was a tree brought into the village in springtime to represent the spirit of the fruitful harvest to come. (At the opening ceremonies for the 1998 Winter Olympics in Nagano, Japan, a group of men sang as they raised trees. One Japanese man said he was shocked to see this secret fertility rite performed in front of the entire world.) Another symbol of Western origin was the Green Tree or Green Man. The Green Tree stood for the potent male energy which impregnates Mother Earth with life.

Chinese Taoist tradition links the peach tree with eternal life. Although Buddha disapproved of tree worship, the bodhi or pipal tree under which he meditated and achieved enlightenment is revered by Buddhists in India. In Hindu India, the pipal tree is looked upon as a manifestation of the god Vishnu, and it is forbidden to cut its leaves or branches except for use in acts of worship. For thousands of years the Jews have celebrated the Feast of Tabernacles or *Sukkoth*, marking the end of the harvest season. The *lulog* or palm branch and *ethrog*, the fruit of the citron tree, play key roles in the festivities.

Besides the many oracular trees mentioned in the Old Testament, trees such as the laurel at Delphi were believed to have psychic powers. Connected by its roots with the underworld, the laurel provided access to the foreknowledge of the dead. The oracle of Jupiter in Epirus was situated in a grove of oak trees. There is an old Yaqui Indian tale about a young girl who listened to a talking tree and carried its prophecies to her people. It is not surprising that a recent Disney animation shows the North American Indian woman, Pocahontas, consulting 'Grandmother Willow' for guidance.

The ancient Scythians practised divination with the aid of willow rods – a forerunner of dowsing rods. The Druid priests of the Celts performed their rites in sacred woodlets. The Saxons or early Germans held their ceremonies in the forest as well. In the old Russian province of Moldavia, tree worship was observed for countless generations.

TREES AS THE UNIVERSE, GIVERS OF LIFE, NOURISHMENT, WISDOM AND IMMORTALITY

Trees actually span three worlds. Their branches stretch up to heaven, their roots reach into the underworld, while their trunks and foliage live on the earth. For this reason, trees came to signify both the eternal universe and sacred sustenance in the form of the Tree of Life. Although Qabalists depict the structure of the universe in terms of the Tree of Life, it has, since the most ancient of times, been conveyed in this manner and form throughout the world. Let us now take a closer look at this.

In ancient India, the Tree of Life was the fig, or *Ashwattha*. The Hindu avatar Krishna instructs his pupil Arjuna through the symbolism of this tree in the *Bagavad Gita*. The idea of the tree as the universe was known to the Scandinavians of old in the form of an ash tree called *Yggdrasil*, or World Tree.

Cosmic trees usually bore fruit which the gods and goddesses ate to ensure their immortality, and so became known as trees of life. The Koran tells of an enormous tooba tree covered with different kinds of food growing in the midst of the seventh or highest level of heaven. The juices of the psychedelic Persian *haoma* and Indian *soma*, known as 'the pillar of the World',

were taken to ward off disease, lengthen life and bestow transcendental experiences.

There were also the mystical trees of the Garden of Eden. Tradition states that the Tree of Knowledge of Good and Evil was an apple tree. Although the exact species of the Tree of Life is not disclosed, this representation of perfect harmony and spiritual immortality was probably an evergreen. The ten 'fruits' or spheres in the branches of the Tree of Life are said to be the products of spiritual development. They are believed to be manifestations of the great spirit of life signified by the Crown at the top of the tree. Those who eat the fruits of the Tree of Life or drink an essence extracted from this holy tree are said to receive eternal life.

The Jewish Talmud speaks of two paradises connected by a pillar or ladder, sometimes called 'Jacob's Ladder', which the souls of the righteous ascend on the Sabbath to enjoy the splendour of divine majesty. Similar to this is the Jews' Inverted Tree, which has its roots in heaven and grows down toward the earth. This tree depicts the belief that human life is the descent of spirit into bodily form. Chinese, Native American and South American Indian legends mention both the living and dead climbing to and from heaven up and down the trunk of a tree.

Black Elk, a modern Oglala Sioux visionary, spoke of the Tree of Life within his 'Great Vision for men'. He taught that the roots of the great Tree of Life are still alive in the hearts of each one of us. The Big Tree of Tule, a majestic Montezuma bald cypress, measured at over 121 feet around, presently grows in the churchyard at Santa Maria del Tule in the southern part of Oxaca, Mexico. This giant symbol of eternal life was supposedly planted by the Aztec prophet Pecocha in the sixth century BC.

Representations of sacred palm, pomegranate and cypress trees are found on Chaldean, Babylonian and Assyrian engravings and temples. In Assyro-Babylonian mythology, the hero

Gilagmesh reached the holy Mount Mashu 'whereon rose the tree of the gods'. Sacred trees of life were also associated with the worship of the gods of the earth and air, Bel and Enlil.

In ancient Egypt the tamarisk was sacred to the god Osiris. Egyptian lore also tells of the sycamore tree. The sycamores existed on the border of this world and the next. On reaching these trees, the souls of the departed would receive supplies of food and water from the spirits dwelling within their foliage.

Finally, one of the chief man-made amusements at Disney's recently completed Animal Kingdom is a huge Tree of Life that lights up at night.

TREES AS SACRED LADDERS

As a child I remember how, when I climbed a tree, I felt safer from the real and imaginary dangers on the earth below because I believed that I was closer to heaven. Trees or ladders have performed similar functions in many traditions. One of the best known is Jacob's Ladder, spoken of in Genesis 28:12. 'And Jacob lay down ... and he dreamed, and beheld a ladder set up on the earth, and the top of it reached to heaven; and he beheld the angels of God ascending and descending on it.'

In the ancient Persian cult of Mithra, initiates were said to have climbed a seven-rung ladder to the heavenly realms. The Prophet Mohammed's famed ascent to heaven on horseback is considered to be via another type of ladder.

The Native American medicine man or woman is said to ascend a sacred rainbow serpent whose seven colours represent the seven levels of heaven. Seven-storied, many-coloured ziggurats or pyramids were prominent in the Babylonian, Egyptian, Mayan, and Aztec civilizations. Reaching the seventh level was equated with reaching the summit of the cosmos.

As a part of their rites, certain sects of oriental monks are said to climb a ladder built of swords in their bare feet. The ascent of a living birch tree plays an important role in the initiation ceremonies of Siberian shamans. The tree, which is rooted in the earth and projects through the smoke hole of the yurt or dwelling, is believed to bridge the way to the spirit world for those who get to its top.

WHAT IS THE QABALISTIC TREE OF LIFE?

As stated in the first section, when the word 'Qabalah' is spelled with the letter Q it represents an *inclusive* tradition that is not limited to or associated with a specific religious denomination. Therefore the Qabalistic Tree of Life presents a harmonious blending of the wisdom traditions of both the East and West. This Tree of Life depicts the principle that there are as many ways to know the divine as there are people on the face of the earth, and that each person will achieve this knowledge in his/her own particular way and time. This concept may be seen in the numerous paths leading to the tree's top. It is helpful to have a picture of the Tree of Life in front of you while reading the following section (see Figures 1 and 4).

A COMPUTER, MAP AND CHART

The Qabalistic Tree of Life is a cosmic computer. Like the computer, the Tree of Life will interact with both beginners and experts. Both the computer and Tree of Life are filing systems for storing enormous amounts of information which, through time and training, become more accessible. The Tree of Life and the computer also mirror the mind and imagination of those who interact with it.

The Qabalistic Tree of Life is a map of divine and human consciousness. It plots the unending journey between spirit and matter. Spirit changes into matter by involution – movement from the Crown at the top of the Tree to the Kingdom at the bottom. Matter changes into spirit by evolution – movement from the Kingdom at the bottom of the Tree to the Crown at its top. Because it represents both the cosmic and personal experience of life, the Tree of Life is thought of as both a constantly transforming and a stable reality. This remarkable symbol offers us a systematic approach to life because it diagrams the development of human consciousness while we live in the physical world and body.

The Qabalistic Tree of Life is a graphic presentation of the interactions that occur between universal and personal consciousness. The very structure of the Tree of Life shows how the human personality is brought into a conscious relationship with the greater impersonal Self. In this sense, the Tree functions as a chart of our step-by-step mastery of the universal forces that surround us and play through our lives.

Because the Tree of Life is a picture of the various stages through which people mature to achieve higher consciousness, it makes the powers and abilities that result from spiritual evolution perceptible. Here it becomes important to remember that what we understand is always a reflection of our level of awareness at one particular time. Therefore, you may contemplate the Tree of Life today and see it one way, while at another time you might comprehend it quite differently.

Finally, although seemingly contradictory to the idea of Oneness, the Tree of Life identifies the ten facets of the one godhead and shows how these facets are really one and the same.

A PARADIGM OF CREATION

Whether Hebrew, Christian or Universal in origin, the Tree of Life is a paradigm of creation. It lays out the ten steps that characterize the process of creation – the unfolding of the hidden

62   and unknowable godhead into the 'fullness' of the manifest
godhead by way of the physical world and its creatures. In this
sense, the Tree of Life is a mandala of life.

The Qabalistic Tree of Life is like a cosmic Christmas tree: its
ornaments are the joys and sorrows of daily life, and its gifts are
the love, wisdom and understanding that come to us through
our life experiences. The Tree of Life is truly unique, as it is a
physical form where every human feeling, thought, and experience may be placed, identified and understood.

THE DIVINE PLAN

A plan is a detailed scheme that shows us how to go about achieving a particular goal. Although each person's goals differ, our goal
as a race is to discover and live out our soul's purpose with as
much wisdom, understanding and love as we are capable of.

Qabalistic lore tells us that the Qabalah is a gift from the Most
High to humanity. The Qabalah's teachings have been transmit-
ted to us through angels and wise ones for thousands of years.
The Qabalah, by way of the Tree of Life and the principles
encoded with it, offers guidelines that may help us to live in
harmony with the divine, our human sisters and brothers, the
planet and the rest of creation. This symbol also charts ways
to better play our personal roles in the world, and by doing so,
to achieve higher consciousness. For these reasons the Qabalah
and Tree of Life are considered to be a divine plan.

Although many books attempt to explain the divine plan,
none is quite so revealing as the insights and information that
arise from one's personal contemplation of the Tree of Life. Taking the time to do this is very rewarding, since it can unveil
the mysteries which are part of its structure. Most important,
the information that is revealed in this way is *always* relevant to
what a person needs to become aware of at that moment.

Studying and applying the principles of the Qabalah through the Tree of Life are intended to bring you into an intimate relationship with your higher Self and the godhead. Through this closeness, you begin to truly understand the divine plan – in terms of who and what you really are and your place in the world.

A GUIDED TOUR OF THE QABALISTIC TREE OF LIFE

YOU ARE THE TREE OF LIFE!

Before we look at the Qabalistic Tree of Life as a representation of the greater impersonal universe and such disciplines as the tarot and astrology, let us contemplate its personal side. This point of view shows us the exciting truth that each human being is a Tree of Life and that the Tree is a living, breathing being.

Qabalists have superimposed the body of Adam Kadmon (Figure 2), symbol of 'Every Human', on the Tree of Life for countless generations. The reason that the body appears backward and sexless is to show that it is, in fact, *Every* Human. Because the Tree of Life also represents the cosmos, the Tree of Life in human form is a simple way of showing us that we are made in the likeness of our cosmic parents.

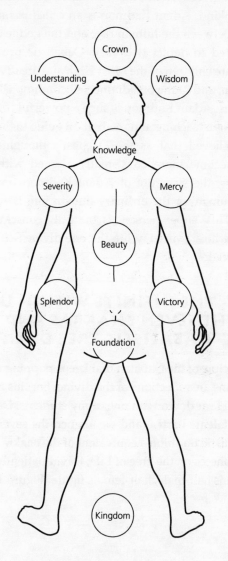

Figure 2 Adam Kadmon, symbol of 'Every Human', shows that we are made in the likeness of our cosmic parents.

Like other great systems, the Qabalah asserts the infinite nature of humankind. Adam Kadmon is an *actual picture* of the relationship between the human race and the godhead. This figure was created to depict two basic Qabalistic principles: 1) we humans are children of the Most High and are divine in essence and origin; and 2) the one divine Self continuously lives in and through us. Adam Kadmon is such a powerful concept that it is still used as a teaching and meditation guide to this day.

It is believed that as the Qabalist's thoughts, words and actions become more consistently aligned with higher consciousness, the structure of Adam Kadmon transforms from 'Every Human' or the ordinary human into the extraordinary human. This 'super person' is the fully conscious individual through whose everyday life the one divine Self may actually be perceived.

THE INFINITE WITHIN US:
THE SEVEN CHAKRAS AND THE
QABALISTIC TREE OF LIFE

One principle of the Qabalah that keeps popping up asserts that we humans are reflections of the divine. For this reason, several years ago I sat down with one of my students, David Boulting-house, a talented artist, and we aligned the seven inner stars – the Qabalistic tradition's equivalent of the chakra system – with the ten spheres on the Tree of Life. David patiently and lovingly created this half-male, half-female figure (Figure 3).

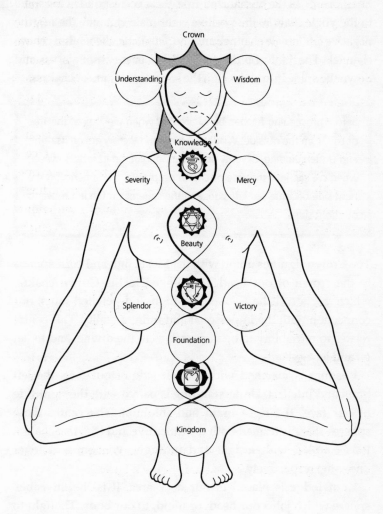

Figure 3 The Tree of Life in human form.

PRINCIPLES OF QABALAH

68   The Qabalistic Tree of Life has three pillars: Mercy, Severity and Equilibrium. In the humanized Tree, these correspond in the spine to the yogic *Pingala*, the positive right male channel; the *Ida*, the negative left female channel; and the *Shushuma*, the neutral central channel. The Holy Spirit, or *Kundalini* energy, spirals up and down the spine in and through the seven inner stars or chakras.

> Before proceeding further, be aware that when we look at the Tree of Life from the outside, Wisdom, Mercy and Victory are on its right, and Understanding, Severity and Splendour are on its left. However, when we slip into the Tree of Life to *become* it, the spheres on the right side become *our* left side, and the spheres on the left move to our right side.

The **Crown** signifies union with the Most High and corresponds to the crown of our head. It is linked to the Crown chakra, which yogis call the *Sahasrar*, or thousand-petalled lotus, our connection with the impersonal and infinite reality. This centre relates to our ability to open ourselves to the divine, and to 'let go and let God'.

Wisdom is matched with the left side of our face, the left brain and intellect. **Understanding** is paired with the right side of our face, the right brain and intuition. The centre these spheres share is termed both the Inner Eye and the *Ajna* chakra. It is coupled with insight and foresight, wisdom and inner knowing, respectively.

Knowledge is placed in our neck area. It is the 'invisible' sphere which joins our head, or mind, to our body. Thought to be a blending of Wisdom and Understanding, Knowledge is situated at the gap between these spheres. Because the very early texts state that there are only *ten* spheres on the Tree of Life, many Qabalists do not recognize its existence.

In approximately this same latitude reside **Mercy**, our permissive left arm, and **Severity**, our protective right arm. Knowledge, Mercy and Severity correspond to our neck and the Throat centre. The *Visuddha* chakra is associated with creative self-expression, how we receive communication and communicate our ideas and imaginings to others. This centre is also related to our values in such forms as kindness and charity, the types of behaviour that we find acceptable and unacceptable, our willingness to aid and protect those who cannot do so for themselves, and fear of what will happen to us when we purposefully harm others. The fact that this centre is also influenced by Knowledge, suggests how Knowledge of God and higher truth can potentially influence how we behave.

Beauty resides in the middle of our chest, the Heart centre, or *Anahata* chakra. It is conjoined with unconditional love, spiritual devotion and intoxication, and who we are 'at heart'. It is not surprising that Qabalists refer to this centre as the Redeemer Within.

Linked to our Solar Plexus centre, or *Manipura* chakra, are **Victory** and **Splendour**, our left and right hips and legs, respectively, which indicate how we, as the human personality, go about asserting ourselves in order to achieve our desires and plans.

Foundation is our Reproductive centre or *Svadhisthana* chakra, the male and female sex glands and organs. This centre is associated with our sex drive and the energy needed to reproduce our species – our biological lust for life and the passion of the Most High coursing through all living things. It also has to do with our automatic use of these same forces to mobilize our bodies in order to manifest our dreams, plans and creative yearnings.

Finally, Kingdom is aligned with our Root centre, or *Muladhara* chakra, located at the base of our spine. It is also conjoined with our organs of elimination and feet. This centre pertains to our sense of physical security and ability to meet our essential bodily needs. It also refers to how connected we are to our physical world, body and other people as well as our capacity to accept and work within the constraints natural to physical form and human society. Because this chakra corresponds to our eliminative organs it relates to how easily we dispose of material possessions that are no longer useful.

TEN SHINING JEWELS

The word *sephiroth* refers to all ten circles on the Tree of Life, while the term *sephirah* refers to each individually. The root of these words, *seph*, translates from the Hebrew to mean 'a shining jewel or emanation'. The terms *sephiroth* and *sephirah* are more commonly interpreted as 'spheres' and 'sphere', respectively.

Pronunciation of the Names of the Sephiroth on the Tree of Life

The word 'Sephiroth' is used when referring to *all* the spheres or emanations on the Tree of Life at once:

Sephiroth   Sef-hear-oht*

The word 'Sephirah' is used when referring to *one* of the emanations or spheres on the Tree of Life:

Sephirah   Sef-hear-rah

English	Hebrew	Phonetic
Crown	Kether	Keh-ter
Wisdom	Chokmah	Hoak-ma
Knowledge	Daath	Da-aht
Understanding	Binah	Bee-na
Mercy	Chesed	Heh-said
Severity	Geburah	Geh-boor-ah
Beauty	Tiphareth	Tiff-are-et
Victory	Netzach	Net-zahk

Splendour	Hod	Ha-odd
Foundation	Yesod	Yes-odd
Kingdom	Malkuth	Mal-koo-t

* The 'th' sound is pronounced as 't'. The 'h' is barely audible.

THE THREE PILLARS, TIME AND ENERGY

Each of the three pillars on the Tree of Life represents a segment in time and type of energy (Figure 4). The Crown heads the middle column, called the Pillar of Equilibrium, which signifies the present moment and stabilized or neutral energy. This middle pillar is about synergy, the new force created when the activities of the two other pillars and the pairs of opposing sephiroth blend and work together. The Pillars of Mercy and Severity, which signify the positive and negative or masculine and feminine polarities respectively, originate from the Crown at the top of the neutral Pillar of Equilibrium.

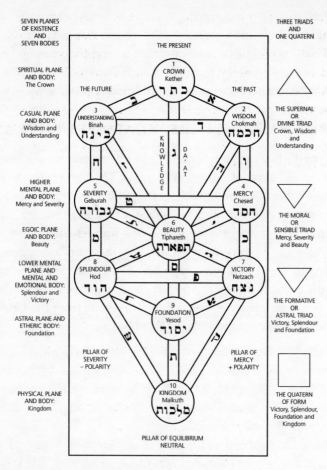

SEVEN PLANES
OF EXISTENCE
AND
SEVEN BODIES

SPIRITUAL PLANE
AND BODY:
The Crown

CASUAL PLANE
AND BODY:
Wisdom and
Understanding

HIGHER
MENTAL PLANE
AND BODY:
Mercy and Severity

EGOIC PLANE
AND BODY:
Beauty

LOWER MENTAL
PLANE AND
MENTAL AND
EMOTIONAL BODY:
Splendour and
Victory

ASTRAL PLANE AND
ETHERIC BODY:
Foundation

PHYSICAL PLANE
AND BODY:
Kingdom

THREE TRIADS
AND
ONE QUATERN

THE SUPERNAL
OR
DIVINE TRIAD
Crown, Wisdom
and
Understanding

THE MORAL
OR
SENSIBLE TRIAD
Mercy, Severity
and Beauty

THE FORMATIVE
OR
ASTRAL TRIAD
Victory, Splendour
and Foundation

THE QUATERN
OF FORM
Victory, Splendour,
Foundation and
Kingdom

THE PRESENT

THE FUTURE   THE PAST

1
CROWN
Kether
כתר

3
UNDERSTANDING
Binah
בינה

2
WISDOM
Chokmah
חכמה

KNOWLEDGE   DA'AT

5
SEVERITY
Geburah
גבורה

4
MERCY
Chesed
חסד

6
BEAUTY
Tiphareth
תפארת

8
SPLENDOUR
Hod
הוד

7
VICTORY
Netzach
נצח

9
FOUNDATION
Yesod
יסוד

PILLAR OF
SEVERITY
– POLARITY

PILLAR OF
MERCY
+ POLARITY

10
KINGDOM
Malkuth
מלכות

PILLAR OF EQUILIBRIUM
NEUTRAL

Figure 4 The Qabalistic Tree of Life. How its three pillars relate to time and energy. Dividing the Tree into the three triads and one quatern. The seven planes of existence and seven bodies.

Wisdom heads the Pillar of Mercy and signifies the past, what has already come into existence. This pillar not only symbolizes the positive polarity which is projective in nature, but also masculine or yang energy, as it is called in oriental traditions.

Understanding crowns the Pillar of Severity which signifies what will come into existence in the future. This pillar is associated with the negative polarity which is receptive in nature, the feminine or yin energy, that is the counterpart to the yang force.

Although a sephirah is set on a particular pillar, it helps you to be aware that *each* sephirah has both projective and receptive qualities. This concept is illustrated by the way each sephirah sends and receives energy through the paths running to and from the surrounding sephiroth.

THREE THREES, ONE FOUR AND A SET OF SEVEN

Besides exploring the Qabalistic Tree of Life's three triads and one quatern, we will take a closer look at the metaphysical system of the seven planes of existence and seven bodies, briefly mentioned earlier (Figure 4).

THE SUPERNAL OR DIVINE TRIAD

Looking at the Qabalistic Tree of Life, we see how the Crown, Wisdom and Understanding form a triangle. This formation is called the Supernal, Heavenly or Divine Triad. As its name implies, this triad makes up the godhead.

The Supernal Triad symbolizes the divine forces and Universal Mind which create the substance from which the manifest world is made. This grouping is equated with both the Holy Spirit and the essential Self. This Triad is sometimes referred to as the Qabalistic Trinity of the Most High, Father God, and Mother Goddess; the Crown, Wisdom and Understanding, respectively.

The Crown stands alone on the Spiritual Plane, reiterating the principle that there is only One Great Spirit and all life springs, or in Qabalistic terms, *emanates*, from this Spirit.

Although Wisdom and Understanding originate from the same point of unity in the Crown, these spheres coexist on the Causal Plane. Cause initiates effect, therefore the Causal Plane is associated with creative *possibilities* or *tendencies*.

THE MORAL OR SENSIBLE TRIAD

Mercy, Severity and Beauty shape the Moral, Sensible or Ethical Triad. Notice that the Moral Triad mirrors the Supernal Triad above. This shows how the spiritual principles of the higher world are brought into the material world through the human race. Life as we know it evolves from the universal substance sent from the Supernal Triad, and the Moral Triad represents the powers in charge of governing and protecting this life by way of human value systems. Therefore, this triad relates to those laws and principles that alleviate suffering and assist humanity's spiritual advancement. The Moral Triad presents us with the precepts that help us to live righteous lives – lives lived with a clear conscience. Because Mercy and Severity sit on the Higher Mental Plane, these spheres refer to highly aware people who convey the metaphysical Wisdom and Understanding that they receive from the Supernal Triad above into the physical world.

Beauty, the tip of the Moral Triad, is on the Egoic Plane. Ordinarily use of the word 'ego' brings to mind concepts of conceit and that of an individual as the centre and object of all experience. However, in Qabalah the term 'ego' means the source of divine individuality which exists within every human being – the higher Self. On the Qabalistic Tree of Life this is shown by setting Beauty directly under the Crown on the middle pillar.

Because Beauty is placed below Mercy and Severity, this does not mean that one who operates at this level of awareness is any less capable than those on the Higher Mental Plane, only that one has achieved one's awareness more *recently*.

The Moral Triad is related to the thoughts, words and actions expressed by extraordinary or enlightened human beings, who serve as role models for others to follow. It is for this reason that the Moral, Sensible or Ethical Triad refers to the saints, wise ones, masters and adepts, who continuously *know* themselves to be serving as vehicles though which the sacred spirit lives and works.

THE FORMATIVE OR ASTRAL TRIAD

Victory, Splendour and Foundation comprise the Formative or Astral Triad. As its name tells us, this triad stands for the pre-material forms from which the physical world is made. Like the Moral Triad above, this arrangement also mirrors the Supernals. While the Moral Triad signifies the super-aware or extraordinary human beings, this Triad is associated with the average person, who is slowly but surely evolving to higher or enlightened consciousness.

Situated on the Lower Mental Plane, the spheres of Victory and Splendour correspond to the feeling and thinking of the average person. This is someone who, in some instances, is unaware of what he/she is saying and doing – he/she is on automatic – yet at other times is completely Self-aware. The Lower Mental Plane is seated between the Upper Mental and Astral Planes. The non-physical planes form the underpinnings of the material world. This placement shows us that the human personality receives input from the higher Self, above, as well as the personal subconscious and the collective unconscious below. That is, thoughts and actions may stem directly from the part of our mind which is exempt from immediate conscious awareness and from our being a part of the human race as a whole – the personal subconscious and collective unconscious, respectively.

Forming the final angle of this triad, Foundation, on the Astral or Psychic Plane, is most often associated with instincts,

impulses and automatic habits. Therefore, it relates to our personal subconscious and to the collective unconscious. As it sits upon the middle pillar, Foundation receives, clarifies and balances the energies of the sephiroth from above and beneath it.

Because our thoughts and feelings are 'things', the Astral Triad generates the prematerial or intangible patterns that, depending upon circumstances, might manifest in material form. This triad serves as the conduit through which spirit enters the physical world and matter exits. It is further linked with the mental and emotional forces from which we humans co-create the world around us. This may help us to better understand why the Astral or Formative Triad accounts for the third step in the soon-to-be-discussed creative process – our formulating and refining mental and emotional patterns.

THE QUATERN OF FORM

The word 'Quatern' means four, and this four-aspected configuration is made up of Victory, Splendour, Foundation and Kingdom. As you can see, it adds the tenth and final sphere, Kingdom, to bring what is 'formative' or astral and nonphysical, into form. The Quatern of Form is where the life force is stabilized and restricted until it is released by physical death. As the last point in the Quatern, Kingdom, located on the Physical Plane, is the sphere most associated with the entire material world, the birth of living bodies and their inevitable decay and death. Finally, the presence of Kingdom within the Quatern of Form tells of the fourth step in the creative process – physical manifestation. More about the four-fold process of creation follows.

CREATION À LA QABALAH

We will now explore the four steps in the creative process – emanation-ideation, imagination, formulation and physical manifestation.

Creation, from the Qabalistic point of view, can potentially help you become more aware of how the creative process operates, gain awareness of where you may be stuck in a creative undertaking, and/or provide insight to the question of 'What comes next?' regarding a project.

Within the design of the Tree of Life are the four Qabalistic worlds. They are the steps or stages in the process of physical manifestation that take place on both the universal and personal levels. In other words, by learning about the four Qabalistic worlds or stages of creation, you will see how we humans create in much the way that the godhead creates.

THE TETRAGRAMMATON AND CREATION

Because Qabalists believe that the divine is the source of all, the four worlds are not only ordered in four successive steps, they are attributed to four letters of the Tetragrammaton. The Holy Tetragrammaton or four-lettered name of the Most High, YHVH – *Yod, Heh, Vav, Heh*, means *That* which was, *That* which is, and *That* which shall always be. In Qabalah, the Tetragrammaton is also known as 'The Word', the primordial cosmic vibration or big bang that brought forth the physical elements making up creation, and from these, the entire manifest world.

The Tetragrammaton shows the four worlds to be the stages through which spirit evolves to become matter. The function of each letter of the Tetragrammaton and the Qabalistic world it is paired with is further described by the four elements – fire, water, air and earth. Much like a layer cake, *each* sphere on the Qabalistic Tree of Life exists in all four worlds.

THE FIRST QABALISTIC WORLD

The first world is called the World of Archetypes, or *Atziluth*, in Hebrew. This is the divine world of the Universal Mind which generates the seed ideas after which things are then patterned by people and nature. The World of Archetypes corresponds to the first letter of the Tetragrammaton, *Yod*, the element of fire, and is represented by a wand. This world is symbolized by the divine spark that causes the outward and downward flow of emanations or the life force from above. The World of Archetypes may be equated with the state of matter which corresponds to subatomic particles, atoms and electrons.

THE SECOND QABALISTIC WORLD

The second world, the World of Creative Potential, is also called *Briah*. It is linked to the first *Heh* in the Tetragrammaton, the water element, and is designated by a cup. This world is associated with creative possibilities, which are generated by our imagination, dreams and fantasies. This world is linked to the molecular state.

THE THIRD QABALISTIC WORLD

The third world, is known as the World of Mental Formulation, or *Yetzirah*. We may have much inspiration and creative potential; however, unless we are willing to *act*, that is, to consciously commit ourselves to a plan of action that will bring forth what we desire to manifest, our ideas and imaginings will never become physical reality. Therefore, the World of Mental Formulation is associated with refinement – the mental dissection, analysis and reasoning that eliminating extraneous material in order to make decisions and map out plans of action. No wonder this third world is signified by the sword. *Yetzirah* is aligned with the element of air and the Hebrew letter *Vav*, meaning 'a link or connection', from the Tetragrammaton, because the World of Mental

Formulation is what links the invisible and visible worlds. It is coupled with both the gaseous and liquid states.

THE FOURTH QABALISTIC WORLD

The fourth and final world, the World of Manifestation, or *Assiah*, contains completed products or finished works, the physical world, and its physical bodies that are made real through physical action. This world is also linked with the element of earth and the final *Heh* in the name of the Most High. It is the birth of what was conceived in the three worlds above and, therefore, it holds the tangible products of inspiration, creative imagination and mental formulation. The World of Manifestation is characterized by a coin and corresponds to the state of solid forms.

THE FOUR QABALISTIC WORLDS OF CREATION

World	Function	Hebrew Letter	Element	Symbol	Form of Matter
Archetypes	Ideation	Yod	Fire	Wand	Subatomic particles, atoms and electrons
Creative potential	Imagination	Heh	Water	Cup	Molecules
Mental formulation	Discrimination	Vav	Air	Sword	Gases and liquids
Physical manifestation	Physical action	Heh	Earth	Coin	Solids

THE FOUR QABALISTIC WORLDS IN ACTION

Here is an example of this fourfold process at work. On an early spring morning, I sit in my kitchen sipping peppermint tea and looking out at my overgrown backyard. I get the idea to plant a garden. The sparking of the *idea* of a garden is the first World of Archetypes, *Atziluth*. Then I fantasize what I will plant: sweet peas, gardenias, zinnias, mangoes, papayas, lilacs, summer squash, lettuce, tomatoes and watermelons, all on the cool and foggy central California coast. This unrestricted flow of emotionally-motivated imagining is the World of Creative Potential, *Briah*. Next, I go outside, examine the soil, think about the climate and the amount of space genuinely available for planting. Critical thinking or analysis enables me to place certain limits on my ideas and imaginings – I had best eliminate what reason tells me will not grow – and settle the unsettled elements. I decide to exclude the mangoes, papayas, lilacs and watermelons. The World of Mental Formulation helps me to plan better and thereby manifest my garden.

Finally I prepare the soil, plant, water, weed, cultivate, get out of bed at 2am to de-snail the seedlings and set my cats out to feast on gophers. Before long I have lettuce for salad and zinnias for the dinner table. The hands-on *physical work* and its resulting products are the fourth and final plane on the Qabalistic Tree of Life, *Assiah*, the World of Manifestation.

SEVERAL POINTS OF VIEW

The sephiroth are thought of in several different ways.

First, the sephiroth are the Most High God manifest. Each sephirah represents a different aspect of the Most High. For this reason, you may think of them as the infinite in finite form. The sephiroth are aspects of the Most High which were expressed in order, from one to ten, as the first sephirah, the Crown, emanated outward and downward from on high. This occurrence is often expressed in the parable of Adam's descent from heaven to earth. In the Qabalah Adam represents the entire human race. The ten spheres show the ten facets of the Most High God and how these facets are not only interrelated, but at a basic level are one and the same.

Secondly, the sephiroth symbolize our own divinity. Because we humans are made in the image of our divine parents, the sephiroth symbolize our sacred essence and origin. In this sense, the sephiroth embody the ancient Hermetic axiom, 'As above, so below'.

Thirdly, the sephiroth are tools that assist us to understand and to ascend the ladder of spiritual evolution. The spheres are tools or particular types of divine consciousness – Wisdom, Understanding, Mercy and Severity and so on. As we develop and live out these archetypes, we develop an intimate and loving relationship with the divine presence within ourselves, with one another, and with the world around us. As a bonus, we mature spiritually. The idea that each sephirah represents a step on the ladder of spiritual development will again be explored under the Graded Tree of Life.

Fourth, the sephiroth *signify* **all change and the unchangeable.** The sephiroth are 'vessels' in and through which all change in the universe takes place and 'light', the one divine power, which is unchangeable. (The Qabalah offers many a paradox!)

PURE EXISTENCE OR NOTHINGNESS

The first sephirah, named the Crown or *Kether* in Hebrew, is placed at the top and 'crowns' the Tree of Life. However, behind the Crown or Most High God lies Pure Existence or Nothingness, the *potential* behind all life and creativity and from which each and every thing originates.

The Crown is said to have come into being from Pure Existence through a three-staged developmental process. These stages, often referred to as Veils of Negative Existence, are given the Hebrew names *Ain*, Pure Nothingness; *Ain Soph*, The Limitless Nothingness; and *Ain Soph Aur*, The Limitless Light, in order of their increasing density. The term 'Negative Existence' is used because they transcend space and time and have no specific qualities.

The following ideas may help you to better understand this concept. In mathematics the term 'negative' pertains to a quantity less than zero, and Negative Existence is the stage of creation *prior* to its actual beginning. Also, another meaning of the word negative is neutral, and to neutralize suggests that Negative Existence is a perfectly balanced state in which the positive and negative polarities as we ordinarily know them, do not occur.

THE CROWN:
ETERNAL, ENDLESS AND CHANGELESS

As mentioned, the Crown or *Kether* sits alone on the Spiritual Plane. Because the Crown represents the godhead gathering Itself into Itself before expressing Itself in the form of creation, it is the only sephirah on the Spiritual Plane. The Crown is the eternal, endless, changeless and everlasting light of consciousness. This 'light' is not light as we know it, but the pure radiant energy which has no mass or electrical charge yet is able to create protons and electrons, the building blocks of atoms, and, therefore, the universe.

The Crown is the One that is in All, and the All that is in the One, the absolute, infinite and undifferentiated Oneness that becomes all of existence. This sephirah stands for the Primal Will of the Most High God, which contains the plan of the universe in its entirety. The Crown symbolizes the Primordial Ground or cosmic substance from which all comes. It is the indivisible and indestructible essence of existence beyond all matter or even anti-matter, all phenomena, all change, and all becoming. This sphere symbolizes the cosmic paradox – that which is and yet is not. The Crown is the uncreated that precedes all creation, the potential of all things.

The activities of the Crown have been compared to winding up the great clock of life before it begins to run. In reality, the powers of consciousness always spiral inward before they move outward. This may be likened to our turning inward to gather energy and formulate a plan of action, before we act.

Some Qabalists do not include the Crown among the sephiroth, thinking that it is not an actual emanation of the Most High, but *is* the Most High God. The Crown is placed at the head of the sephiroth, as it *is* the source of all. It represents the one pure spirit, the one vital principle or animating force behind and within the entire living world. This sephirah stands for the Absolute Unity, the Great 'Isness' from which proceed the masculine and feminine principles, which are also termed the positive and negative polarities.

WISDOM AND UNDERSTANDING: FATHER AND MOTHER OF MATTER

When I explained the Principle of Polarity, I stated that Father God and Mother Goddess, or Wisdom and Understanding,

respectively, spring from the Most High, the Crown sephirah. For this reason, the godhead is *both* male and female in nature. Furthermore, everything that exists is believed to be the result of the coupling of divine maleness and divine femaleness, the positive and negative polarities.

Both the second and third sephiroth, Wisdom and Understanding, are fixed upon the Tree of Life's Causal Plane. The second sephirah, Wisdom or *Chokmah*, as he is called in Hebrew, is the tangible reflection of the Crown. Wisdom is the Father of Matter, the divine Word or Logos that ushers the universe into being. Wisdom projects all the life-giving energy received from the Crown into the third sephirah, the Mother of Matter, Understanding or *Binah*, as she is known in Hebrew.

Mother Goddess or Understanding is the great womb of life into which the undifferentiated cosmic energy from Wisdom flows. Within this sephirah, this non-specific energy separates into specific forms and is given its Holy Soul, or *Neshamah*. The interaction of these twin forces may be likened to cutting out cookies from a sheet of dough. Wisdom, the cosmic father delivers the dough, the undifferentiated cosmic substance, to Understanding, the cosmic mother and pattern maker. She, in her role as Mother Nature applies her various moulds – human, animal, plant, and mineral – to the dough, and so shapes the world as we know it. Because what is finite endures for only a limited time, entry into the life cycle gives rise to the decay, death and dissolution of that particular form. For this reason, Understanding is the great womb from which life as we know it comes and later returns.

The mating dance of Wisdom with Understanding brings forth finite forms from the infinite reality. Wisdom and Understanding reside on the Causal Plane. This plane brings about the *effect* of physical reality.

The parallel forces of Wisdom and Understanding appear opposite, yet are, in reality, aspects of the same being. Wisdom is the active drive which unites with Understanding, the receptive and formative feminine principle in order to bring about physical reality. Wisdom stimulates and enlivens the dormant creative substance of Understanding. Their interaction demonstrates how creativity is the interchange of these complementary forces.

AN ALTERNATING CURRENT

From the interrelationship between Wisdom and Understanding comes not only the rest of the Tree of Life, but all the rest of life. The whole universe is produced from the tension between the polarities. Qabalists describe this occurrence as follows: The source, the Crown, gives forth a current, Wisdom, which turns into a sea, Understanding, which flows into seven streams, the remaining sephiroth. From this, we see that each sephirah has both inflowing/receptive and outflowing/active energies, or runs on AC, alternating current.

This bipolarity explains how numerous religious and mythological references personify Wisdom, the male principle, as the female principle in forms such as Sophia, Greek goddess of Wisdom. It also shows us: 1) the importance of adopting receptive and active attitudes in order to become wise; and 2) the value of studying each sphere from both views.

FROM THE INVISIBLE
COMES THE VISIBLE:
THE PRINCIPLE OF KNOWLEDGE

Knowledge, or *Da'ath* as it is called in Hebrew, is the 'invisible' sephirah located on the central pillar at the gap or what is termed the 'Abyss', between Wisdom and Understanding just above Mercy and Severity. As mentioned earlier, many

Qabalists do not recognize the existence of this sphere because the ancient Hebrew writings state, 'there are only ten sephiroth, not nine and not eleven, but ten'. However, those who do not include the Crown among the ten sephiroth, regard Knowledge to be the third sephirah.

Generally, Knowledge is thought to be a combination of Wisdom and Understanding that functions as a *bridge*, linking the spiritual and material worlds. Knowledge is not usually placed on one of the seven planes of existence, but it may be considered to span the spiritual and material worlds of the Causal and Higher Mental Planes.

THE COSMIC BIRTH CANAL

Knowledge is believed to be the sphere wherein all the patterns of the spiritual world coalesce into their final forms. Because the word 'knowledge' in the biblical sense means sexual union, the coupling of Wisdom and Understanding is thought to produce this sephirah. Knowledge is often imagined as a cosmic birth canal through which passes what has been conceived from the union of Father God and Mother Goddess into physical reality.

MERCY AND SEVERITY: CONTRASTING PRINCIPLES

Located on the Higher Mental Plane, Mercy and Severity, or *Chesed* and *Geburah* as they are called in Hebrew, bring us into the physical world. We will see how the polarities become increasingly distinct as they descend the Tree of Life into the world of form. Much as the godhead produces the physical polarities that exist throughout nature, it also creates contrasting intellectual principles such as Mercy and Severity. Like the forces of Wisdom and Understanding, Mercy and Severity appear opposed but are two sides of the same coin.

The principles of Mercy and Severity are *best* enacted from an impartial or dispassionate state of mind. In this mode of being one puts personal attachments and prejudices aside in order to assume a more objective and impersonal point of view. Mercy is characterized by expansive, forgiving, generous, empathetic and sympathetic behaviours motivated by love and compassion. In its most elevated state, Mercy embodies what Jesus said as he was being crucified, 'Father, forgive them, for they know not what they do'. Also motivated by love and compassion, Severity is characterized by contractive, disciplinary and restrictive behaviours.

When Mercy becomes overly tolerant, indulgent and lazy, Severity steps in forcefully to restore the balance, but *not* to cause undue harm. When Severity translates into excessively rigid or unnecessarily aggressive behaviours, Mercy comes to the rescue by slaying the necessary dragon, and thereby correcting the imbalance.

Although it may cause fear and upheaval, Severity ideally performs acts of loving kindness. Fear can function as a sign warning us to stop and pay attention to what we are doing. At times, feeling fearful is healthy and lack of fear is unhealthy. If, for example, you are about to steal what is not rightfully yours or go into an unknown wilderness area without a map, fearfulness is *very* appropriate!

EXPANSIVE AND CONTRACTIVE

The ideas of Mercy and Severity should not to be taken in their literal sense, but as titles for the permissive and corrective, expansive and contractive aspects of the Universal Mind (originating in the Crown) as it makes itself known through the human mind and the law of Cause and Effect. These principles may be seen in such areas as lawmaking, which is protective, and law enforcement, which is corrective. Together, Mercy and Severity create a code of personal ethics based upon the highest

levels of integrity and love possible for humans. Severity is the discipline and limit-setting that supports us when we must use force to pursue what we believe to be true justice, and it turns against us when we use that same force intentionally to commit harmful acts. People enacting these principles often function like shields. They use their God-given power to defend and protect those who cannot do so for themselves.

SOCIAL RESPONSIBILITY

Mercy and Severity are evident in socially responsible actions. For example, social and economic reforms seek to change policies that worsen excessive inequality by replacing them with new rules that benefit the long-term common good. This idea is being demonstrated by a new organization called Responsible Wealth. Millionaires act to balance the rise in power of large corporations and the growing gap between the rich and the less wealthy.

People who operate in the spheres of Mercy and Severity believe they have a moral and ethical duty to uphold the principle that all people were created equal, and that we were endowed by our Creator with certain unalienable rights. They believe that everyone should have equal rights to such as life, liberty and the pursuit of happiness.

INBORN ABILITY

Because these sephiroth are positioned on the Higher Mental Plane, Mercy and Severity represent the most spiritually evolved level of human intelligence that human beings are capable of while they live in the physical world and body. Those functioning at this level of consciousness have the *inborn* ability to live by their spiritual values. They are receptive to greater Wisdom and Understanding from the spheres above, yet have their feet firmly planted on the earth. Although the human personality is fully operational, it takes its direction from the higher Self.

THE PRINCIPLE OF BEAUTY:
SYNERGY AND HARMONY

Beauty, or *Tiphareth* as it is called Hebrew, is the sixth sephirah or emanation on the Tree of Life. Beauty sits at the centre of the Tree on the Pillar of Equilibrium on the Egoic Plane. The Tree's middle pillar is about synergy, the harmonious new force created when the activities of the two other pillars and pairs of opposing sephiroth blend and work together. Within Beauty the Individual Spirit, called *Ruach*, joins with the Holy Soul or *Neshamah*, which comes from above. The Holy Soul determines whether one is a man or woman, while the Individual Spirit determines the specific personality one is to have.

THE HEART

Because of its location in the Tree's centre or heart, Beauty is connected to all of the other spheres. Like the heart, Beauty pumps the life force (blood) to and from the outlying sephiroth (veins and arteries) thereby supplying the entire Tree of Life (body) with vital energy. Beauty sends, receives and balances the life force within the Tree of Life and human body. Beauty functions like a mediator. It receives and transmits influences and information from on high, the sephiroth above, to our personality, the sephiroth below. Beauty also receives and transmits our prayers and wishes back to our higher Self.

As the human heart, Beauty signifies love and devotion. These may be conditional, meaning that it is only given when another behaves or appears in a particular way. Love and devotion may also be unconditional, and given for the pure sake of loving, without another having to do or be anything but his/her self. For this reason, Beauty is linked with spiritual intoxication, the ecstatic state of loving the divine with complete abandon. In this state we are not only acutely aware that

God is all, but are able to love the divinity that exists in the hearts of all.

Beauty is also about who we are at heart, our genuine character and disposition, the personality traits needed (and many believe selected) for this particular lifetime. Qabalists believe that it is through the human personality and physical body that we enter into physical life to fulfil our spiritual contracts.

This sephirah introduces us to what Qabalists call ego. Ego is the part of us that *knows*, not just thinks, that our personal growth is really an act of responding to 'something greater' than our personal selves. This something greater is our higher or essential Self. The Qabalistic Tree of Life shows us that we are connected to both the spiritual and material worlds because Beauty is connected to all of the sephiroth, both above and below.

LIVING A BEAUTIFUL LIFE

According to an old saying, 'beauty is in the eye of the beholder'. This indicates that what is regarded to be beautiful varies from person to person, since culture, society and experience teach us what is beautiful and what is not. One of the greatest inspirations from contemplating Beauty is to retrain our senses to be aware of the Beauty of the Most High that is present in everything.

Not only is living a beautiful life closely connected with our being able to see the Beauty of the Most High within creatures great and small, but with learning to distinguish right from wrong. For this reason, Beauty is also associated with the human conscience and the power to determine what is right and wrong in our personal behaviour. Beauty is also paired with intuition, which also helps us to know how to best proceed. Intuition is the pure sense of knowing, direct knowledge or certainty arrived at without reason. It emanates from the centre of one's being and resonates in one's heart.

Adam, or every person within whom the one divine consciousness plants the seed of the wise one or Christ, is linked with Beauty. Therefore, Beauty is not only about learning spiritual principles, but putting them into practice daily. Beauty is identified with the concept that we are perfectly imperfect beings who are slowly becoming more perfect or divine by relating to our everyday lives with an increasing awareness of the sacred spirit that pervades physical reality.

THE SAVIOUR WITHIN

In view of this last discussion, it makes sense that Beauty is also the Messiah, the fully conscious or enlightened human personality who redeems us. This state of awareness is called the Christ Consciousness and deification by Western mystics, and Self-Realization, Wakefulness and *Baqa* by yogis, Buddhists and Sufis. The Messiah or Saviour may certainly take the form of an enlightened person, but at this time in the human evolutionary cycle it is more likely to be the enlightened aspect of our personality, which has been inspired by illuminated people and teachings. Simply, it is our own ability to perceive the Beauty of the Most High present in all people, creatures, places, things and situations, that redeems and saves us. When used in the Qabalah, the term 'Christ Consciousness' refers to both Jesus, the Christ, and to the Messiah, the Saviour or Redeemer who lives within each of our hearts.

VICTORY AND SPLENDOUR: COMPLEMENTARY PRINCIPLES

Located on the Lower Mental Plane, Victory and Splendour, or *Netzach* and *Hod* as they are named in Hebrew, like the other pairs of sephiroth, complement one another. This is because Victory, the seventh sephirah, represents our imaginative and passionate feeling-self and Splendour, the eighth, our logical and analytical thinking-self. While we may think we live in the world, we spend a great deal of time living in our thoughts, feelings and imagination.

Located on the Lower Mental Plane, the sephiroth between Victory and Kingdom show us the average human personality. This is not intended to be negative, only to show the difference between ordinary people and the enlightened human beings associated with the spheres above.

Victory is associated with human desire, emotion and imagination that stem from having wishes and goals and feeling our feelings. Splendour is coupled with the human intellect and the reason and logic through which we regulate what we feel and make plans to achieve what we crave. In essence, Victory is the sephirah that enables us to express our feelings, dreams and desires, while Splendour helps us to manage and manifest them intelligently. The interaction between these spheres may be compared with listening to a person speak on the radio and then imagining what they look like or, after feeling attracted to someone at a party, planning how to ask him/her out.

WESTERN CULTURE AND SOCIETY

Although our mind and emotions receive input from the higher and lower sephiroth, Western society often considers the intellect, Splendour, to be superior to emotions, Victory. Yet the ability to feel is as important to our growth on all levels as is the ability to reason. Both are needed to harmonize and unify the personality and to lead healthy and productive lives. Emotion without reason to temper it breeds chaos and insanity, just as mental analysis without feeling breeds an indifference to pleasure and pain that seriously impairs thinking.

'Victory' means one has triumphed over obstacles, yet in the Qabalistic sense, Victory is not attained by 'getting over on another', or purposefully inflicting pain. Victory is a state of harmony, not a state in which one becomes powerful and important at the expense of another. True Victory implies that we are receptive to guidance and direction from our higher soul spirit Self. Victory is also our ability to live out the principle that success is often built upon a foundation of defeats.

To feel splendid is to feel an elevated level of self-respect and approval. We tend to feel splendid when we are mindful, rather than mindless. Mindlessness means that we are not in the here and now, whereas mindfulness brings our full attention to the person, place, thing or situation immediately before us. Of course, the antidote for mindlessness is mindfulness. Therefore, if I have thoughtlessly hurt another's feelings, I can think of ways to make amends and then I do so. As we mature, we become cognizant that when we act respectfully toward ourselves, we are also acting this way toward others, our higher Self and the godhead. Doing this we feel increasingly splendid and others 'magically' tend to respect us more.

Someone especially intelligent is called 'brilliant', another word for Splendour. Through our intellect we come to know and understand ourselves and our place in the scheme of things. Because the human mind is a duplicate of the Universal Mind, it is the most powerful tool on earth. Our rational mind helps to attain what our higher Self desires for us.

WHAT OUR HEARTS' DESIRE

Victory and Splendour are partners. The mind functions as a clearing house for our emotions, and our emotions add life to what reason decides is so. Splendour adds specific details to the emotional force of Victory, and Victory adds passion and

enthusiasm to the ideas born from Splendour. For example, although I sincerely desire to take a trip to Greece, unless I plan how, when, and where to go, I will remain an armchair traveller. On the other hand, I might write an outline for a great new book, but unless I have the passion to do the rest of the work, it will never become a reality. Through the passion and creative imagination of Victory and the intellectual capacity of Splendour, we are helped to realize what our hearts desire.

THE PRINCIPLE OF FOUNDATION

The ninth Sephirah, Foundation, or *Yesod* as it is called in Hebrew, is positioned on the Astral Plane near the bottom of the Pillar of Equilibrium. Like Beauty, Foundation receives, clarifies and blends energies from the spheres above and below. As mentioned, Foundation serves as a conduit through which the influences from on high make their way into physical reality, represented by the sphere of Kingdom. This sephirah also functions like a bank into which all of our personal memories as well as every shared human experience from the beginning of time are deposited. This bank is known as both the personal subconscious and the collective unconscious.

THE INVISIBLE FRAMEWORK BENEATH ALL PHYSICAL FORMS

A Foundation is a base which, in terms of the Qabalistic Tree of Life, is the invisible framework or structure beneath all physical forms, and upon which these are built. I believe this is what physicists mean when they speak of seeing through supposedly stable and solid matter, to perceive the recurrent patterns of light and energy which are in a state of constant flux.

This sephirah fine-tunes and lays out the blueprints for what we have been planning to manifest in the physical world.

Foundation is in charge of the work of incorporation – the consolidation of the mental and emotional patterns conceived in Splendour and Victory into astral blueprints that, in divine time, may be birthed into living things in the sphere of Kingdom.

ASTRAL BLUEPRINTS AND VIRTUAL REALITY

Astral blueprints are much like a computer-generated reality. They conjure up within our minds a simulated or 'virtual reality' through which we may get a sense of what specific things or situations *might* be like before we actually bring them into physical form. Because Foundation is the final evaluation that our ideas and imaginings undergo before they become manifest, we best clarify and correct our potential creations or actions when and where needed.

While it is true that astral blueprints are intangible, they do exist in the suprasensible substance of the astral world above the tangible world. Remember, these prematerial forms are very real despite the fact that they are not yet materialized. Qabalists term the intangible essential energy that enlivens all living creatures, the Vital Soul.

THE ESSENTIAL ENERGY

The Holy Soul, *Neshamah*, and Individual Spirit, *Ruach*, link up with the Vital Soul or *Nefesh*, in Foundation. The Vital Soul is the aspect of the Most High in the form of the basic force of nature that keeps us, and all living creatures, alive or vital. Entry of the Vital Soul into the physical body may be compared to the quickening of life that occurs within each creature that gestates its young.

The Vital Soul is an invisible power that automatically enlivens, connects and coordinates everything in the manifest world. It has been likened to Einstein's theory of the universal gravitational field, an invisible structure that holds everything in the

universe together, and to morphic fields, the invisible organizing structures or blueprints that give all things their coordination, regenerative power and developmental goals. Furthermore, the Vital Soul automatically generates the essential energy needed to sustain life within *all* physical bodies. In humans and animals, these functions include heart rate, respiration, digestion, evacuation, hormone production, gestation and blood circulation.

Qabalists believe the physical world to be a reproduction of our mental world, and Foundation is conjoined with the reproductive organs and womb. The reproductive system holds the instructions that tell our bodies how to reproduce our species and continue life. On the astral level, Foundation provides the essential energy that reproduces what our minds and emotions have begun to shape.

Scott sincerely desires to stop smoking. To do so, he designs a plan of action. First, Scott joins a support group. He also reads books and listens to tapes to sustain his desire and will power. He might find it necessary to examine why he smokes – social pressure, appetite suppression, or to keep unpleasant feelings in check. Perhaps Scott also purchases a nicotine patch or undergoes acupuncture treatments to alleviate his withdrawal symptoms. Along with this course of action, he keeps reproducing a clear mental pattern of himself as a contented non-smoker. Importantly, he makes whatever personal adjustments are necessary to make this image genuine. Eventually his body gets the message and his craving ceases. The consistent duplication of a clarified thought form and actions that reinforce it, illustrates our power to birth ideas into physical form.

Everything that becomes perceptible in Kingdom *must* go through the gestation process in Foundation. For this reason, numerous Qabalists believe Foundation to be a reflection of the

invisible sephirah, Knowledge, which is thought to perform this function for the godhead.

A FOUNDATION IS A SUPPORT

Because a Foundation is also a support, it is associated with the predominant state of our physical, mental and emotional health which, depending upon its state, may support or undermine our living normal lives. If these foundations are unstable, so are we. Because we live in an ever-changing world, the principles of Foundation bring our attention to the value of developing internal support and stability. Both the Eastern and Western traditions teach that equilibrium is the basis or Foundation for the Great Work of spiritual transformation. Founding our lives upon the basic laws and truths of the Qabalah provides vital support to this undertaking.

ASTRAL AND PSYCHIC EXPERIENCES

Foundation sits on the Astral or Psychic Plane and is associated with our astral or etheric body. The ancient Greek and Roman concept of the Underworld or world of the dead is linked with Foundation. Usually we experience this plane in dreams and immediately after the soul leaves the body at death and before birth. Astral or psychic experiences also result from traumatic injuries, mind-altering states or medications that temporarily drive us 'out of our body'. I felt quite unnerved when, after taking a prescription for pain medication for an abscessed tooth, I suddenly began to float over my body while riding home on the bus.

Each major change in our world and personal life is the effect of a cause that begins on the supraphysical planes. Because Foundation is the sephirah immediately before the Physical Plane of Kingdom, psychics, clairvoyants, mediums and the like try to access it in order to foretell the future. Access to

Foundation has also been known to reveal the past, as it contains both personal and group memory, the personal subconscious and collective unconscious.

THE PRINCIPLE OF KINGDOM

The tenth emanation or sephirah, Kingdom, or *Malkuth* as it is called in Hebrew, is seated at the foot of the Pillar of Equilibrium on the Physical Plane. It is the sephirah in which all the forces from the spheres above come together to form one whole and to become the world as we know it. For this reason, Kingdom may be thought of as the downloading of ideas into manifest form. Kingdom is where the life force is temporarily stabilized to become each and every creature and thing. The physical world remains in these forms until decay and death release it into the world of spirit.

Kingdom reiterates the principle that physical reality is spiritual reality thought into form. We and our surroundings are, in truth, reflections and manifestations of the one Self, the Crown. In Kingdom, the statement, 'As above, so below' is fully expressed. Consequently, the name 'Kingdom' means that the Kingdom of Heaven governs and protects the earth. Because all living creatures and things on earth contain the spirit of the Most High, that spirit is the true ruler of the earth plane.

A MAGICAL AND MIRACULOUS PROCESS

The ability to bring something into physical form is a magical and miraculous process. This is particularly true when we are able to see creation for what it really is – spirit in form. As the final step in the sacred process of creation, Kingdom is called the *Shekhinah*, the spirit of the living Most High God on Earth. From this point of view, Kingdom is considered by Qabalists to be the highest level of the developmental process, not the lowest level, as other belief systems teach. The physical world is lowly when we do not perceive it to be spiritual in essence and origin. It is also coarse and vulgar when we are oblivious of what we think, say and do, and fail to recognize the incredible power of our mind to interpret what goes on within and around us. Our minds and emotions are so powerful that when we *think* and *feel* that the world around us is inferior, it becomes so!

> Two friends attend their twenty-year high school reunion and see a classmate who was once a star athlete, now confined to a wheel chair. One immediately becomes undone as she thinks how awful it is that he cannot walk, play sports, and how terrible his life must be. The other thinks, 'The universe works in ways we don't always understand.' While it is very unfortunate that he is unable to use his body as he once did, she notices that he is not only smiling and well dressed but the alumni book lists him as married and a father of twin girls, an attorney who is an advocate for the handicapped, and peer counsellor at the spinal cord unit at a hospital.

ENDINGS AND BEGINNINGS

Although Kingdom is the tenth and final sephirah and suggests the end of the journey, it is also the beginning. This means that our experiences in the physical world eventually inspire our aspirations to higher consciousness and greater spiritual awareness. Inspiration may result from having our physical needs met yet not feeling satisfied, or from being physically deprived and wanting to discover how to work with spirit in order to better care for ourself and loved ones.

Kingdom's placement on the Pillar of Equilibrium suggests that our pilgrimage is often easier when we are physically, mentally and emotionally balanced. This also means that we are not worrying about whether we will die from overexposure to the

cold, when we will next eat, or where we will sleep. Qabalists subscribe to the principle that when we do our best to care for ourselves we tend to be cared for.

REJOICING IN THE WONDER AND DELIGHT

Kingdom is the home of all physical bodies and solid forms. Yet without spirit to enliven it, physical form is nothing more than a lifeless mass of flesh and bones. Looking at the dead body of a human or an animal, you can see this. This sephirah teaches us about rejoicing in the wonder and delight of having a physical body and with it, the five senses. A natural part of our spiritual evolution from the Kingdom back to the Crown is that we become better at using our senses to experience and celebrate the one divine presence within ourselves, one another and the world around us!

THE QABALISTIC INTELLIGENCES

One of the main works of the early Jewish Kabbalah, the *Sepher Yetzirah*, the Book of Formation or Creation, assigns each sephirah and path, the areas between the spheres on the Tree of Life, an Intelligence (Figure 5). Because all is one, and we reflect the One, these Intelligences are another way of describing the powers of the Universal Mind, which, through the development of our mental powers or intelligence, may become a force for us to use at will.

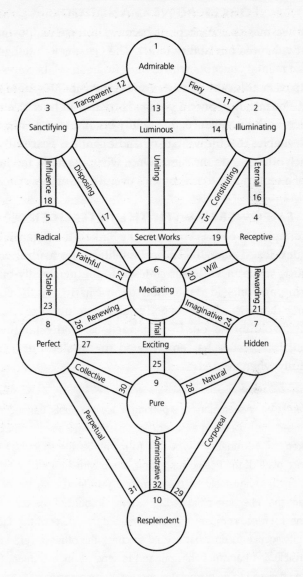

Figure 5 The thirty-two Qabalistic Intelligences

FORCES, POWERS AND TOOLS

When we master a concept, it becomes a force or 'power', in that it enhances our ability to act. The Qabalistic Intelligences are like mental concepts which, once understood, become tools to help us handle our daily lives and responsibilities more effectively. For instance, once a person is trained in how to resolve conflicts without violence, that ability becomes a type of power which enables that individual to handle conflicts peacefully and to teach others to do the same. Once we understand the principles of a sephirah, it too becomes a useful type of power.

EMPOWERED WITH THE INTELLIGENCE

For example, Severity is known as the Radical Intelligence. In its most developed state, the Radical Intelligence is neutral, loving and just, while in its lesser states it is the personally-biased, uncaring, and one-sided intention to cause harm. It is the powerful force that arises from the godhead to revolutionize and ultimately 'evolutionize' our lives and actions. Understanding the Radical Intelligence has empowered me to step out and act forcefully when needed.

Recently, while searching for a parking space in a public parking lot, I noticed a car speeding away after it smashed into an older-model parked car. Fortunately I was able to memorize the short 'vanity' licence plate of the fleeing car. I left it, along with a note to the driver, on the windshield of the damaged vehicle. (Doing this also meant that I became obligated to give my account of the accident to the insurance company.) Simply, I enacted the power of the Radical Intelligence to do what I could to check the other driver's irresponsible and harmful behaviour and to serve as an instrument for what I believed to be the greater good of all concerned.

THE SPIRITUAL EXPERIENCE OF EACH SEPHIRAH

Every human being already has some knowledge of the ten Spiritual Experiences linked with the Tree of Life, or has the potential to know them. For this reason, each of the ten sephiroth is ascribed a particular Spiritual Experience. Such experiences 1) give a deeper meaning to something that is usually not thought of in such a way; and 2) provide a clear sense of divine presence or direction resulting from prayer, meditation, deep concentration, or an altered state of awareness.

The idea of the Spiritual Experience was incorporated into the Qabalistic teachings to let students know that, in time, each of us learns about the principles of a sephirah through direct or extrasensory perception. For this reason, most of the Spiritual Experiences are called 'The Vision of...'. Experiences of this nature help us to understand non-physical or mystical principles.

> The Spiritual Experience of Understanding, *Binah*, is the Vision of Sorrow. These experiences may arise from being in an altered state, and childbirth is certainly such an experience. As I looked into my newborn son's eyes for the first time, I spontaneously had the Vision of Sorrow. During these moments of intense bonding, I was suddenly filled with a mixture of not only unspeakable joy but of great sorrow. I realized, in a nearly indescribable experience, that this tiny person who was just beginning his life would in time age and die. Within seconds, I fully understood, or better yet *experienced* how, when a soul takes on a physical body, it becomes subject to the laws and cycles of nature.

THE TEN SPIRITUAL EXPERIENCES OF THE QABALISTIC TREE OF LIFE

The Crown
Union with the Most High

Wisdom
The Vision of the Most High Face to Face

Understanding
The Vision of Sorrow

Mercy
The Vision of Love

Severity
The Vision of Power

Beauty
The Vision of the Harmony of all Things

Victory
The Vision of Beauty Triumphant

Splendour
The Vision of Splendour

Foundation
The Vision of the Machinery of the Universe

Kingdom
The Vision of the Holy Guardian Angel

ALTERNATIVE TITLES

Calling the same subject by a different name opens us to other points of view and increases the likelihood that we can more fully grasp its meaning. For this reason each sephirah has been given several alternative titles. For example, Mercy is also known as the *Tzaddik*, a Hebrew term that means righteousness, and refers to someone who is a spiritual model – an ideal of moral, social and religious perfection. Corresponding to the ideals of Mercy, the

Tzaddik serves his/her community as the agent or intermediary through which the Most High communicates.

The Celestial Surgeon is an ancient title given to Severity. When personal or worldly conditions are out of balance, the power of Severity descends like a surgeon from on high to operate upon, and thereby eliminate and heal, what is diseased. The fall of the oppressive Eastern European dictatorships shows this principle in action. A listing of alternative titles follows.

The Crown: The Primal Essence. The Still Point. The Primordial Ground. Pure Light of the Void. The Monad. Existence of Existences. Concealed of the Concealed. Ancient of Days. The Most High. Amen. Lux Interna. Lux Occulta. The Vast Countenance. The Sun behind the sun. The Oversoul. *Yekhidah*. Atman. The Head which is Not. The Prime Mover. The Beginning of the Whirlings.

Wisdom: Ab. The Creator. The Supernal Father. The Great Stimulator. The Highway of Life. The Tetragrammaton. *Yod* of the Tetragrammaton. The Principal Thing. 'The Word' or Logos. The Light Force.

Understanding: Ama. Aima. Matronit. The Creatrix. The Supernal Mother. The Triple Goddess. Mater Dolorosa. Mater Bon Consili. *Heh* of the Tetragrammaton. Outer Robe of Concealment. The Great Receiver. Great Multiplier. Giver of the Soul. The Triple Goddess.

Mercy: *Gedulah*. Magnificence. Munificence. Majesty. Master of Compassion. The Tzaddik.

Severity: Justice. Judgement. Strength. Fear. Terror. The Celestial Surgeon. Hall of the Lords of Karma.

Beauty: The Lesser Countenance. The King. The Son and Daughter. The Christ, Messiah, Saviour or Redeemer.

Victory: Success. Fulfilment. Accomplishment. Triumph. Valour. Firmness.

Splendour: Glory. Prudence. Sagacity. Cunning.

Foundation: The Prop. The Stabilizer. The Astral Light. Anima Mundi.

Kingdom: Gate of Tears. The Gate of the Garden of Eden. New Jerusalem. Daughter of the Mighty Ones. The Queen and Bride. The Virgin. The *Shekhinah*.

VIRTUES, VICES AND SOMEWHERE IN-BETWEEN

As is the case with all living things, polarities exist within the ten sephiroth. They are the extremes of behaviour that, within the Qabalistic system, are known as virtues and vices. Although categorizing behaviours in such terms is black and white thinking, a pattern that the Qabalist ultimately wishes to transcend, we can learn many lessons from these distinctions. Our strengths hold the potential to help us to master our weaknesses, and our weaknesses offer us the opportunity to tap into and further develop our strengths.

The ability to acknowledge the existence of the light and dark or positive and negative sides of one's personality has the potential to make us increasingly self-accepting and compassionate, as well as better able to alter our behaviour patterns. In other words, if I am willing to recognize that I have a vice or a negative trait such as codependence, I become open to seeing myself develop its opposite virtues of independence or interdependence. In instances when I catch myself thinking that I am better than someone else because I can enact a certain virtue, I remember that, as a human being, I have the potential to develop its opposite side or vice. By doing this, I contain my 'holier than thou' attitude, keep my feet on the ground, and remember that I have certainly once been where another now stands.

A virtue may also be seen as a behaviour which builds and raises our Self-esteem. Virtues are thoughts, words and actions which preserve, elevate and/or celebrate our own or another's sacred Self. Virtuous behaviours are not only performed for the purpose of doing good works and service, but because we have the conscious desire not to give in to a personal weakness or vice.

A vice tends to undermine and lower our Self-esteem, as it is an indulgence in a personal weakness or immaturity. Vices are thoughts, words or actions that demean, degrade, and/or shame ourselves or others. Vices usually end up hurting those who enact them most.

SHADES OF GREY

When you look at the list of vices and virtues that follows, it helps to remember that they are not completely black and white issues but shades of grey. Because the universe is continuously balancing itself out, every positive or negative action holds the potential to give rise to its opposite and to result in some state in between the two extremes. Therefore, a virtue may turn into a vice and a vice may become a virtue, or create more moderate behaviour. For example, the virtues of the fourth sephirah, Mercy, are obedience and generosity, yet when taken to an extreme these traits may result in blind faith and purposeful or mindless overindulgence. One vice of the fifth sephirah, Severity, is cowardice, which, when modified, can become a healthy respect for what is truly dangerous.

A TABLE OF VIRTUES AND VICES

Sephirah	Virtue	Vice
The Crown	Attainment	None*
Wisdom	Devotion	None
Understanding	Silence	Greed
Mercy	Obedience and Generosity	Gluttony, Bigotry, Tyranny, Hypocrisy and Stinginess

Severity	Courage and Energy	Cowardice, Tyranny, Vengeance and Wanton Destruction
Beauty	Devotion to the Great Work	Pride
Victory	Unselfishness	Lust and Unchastity
Splendour	Truthfulness	Dishonesty
Foundation	Independence and Interdependence	Idleness, Overdependence and Codependence
Kingdom	Discrimination	Inertia

* The Crown lacks a vice because it is not a dual state. Wisdom lacks a vice because it mirrors the Crown.

THE QABALAH AND OTHER SPIRITUAL SYSTEMS

The following segments have the potential to help expand your basic understanding of what the Qabalistic Tree of Life is and how it functions. You will be shown how the Hermetic arts and sciences such as magic, the tarot, astrology, sacred geometry, numerology, mythology and angelogy are part of the Qabalistic system.

ATTRIBUTES, MAGICAL TOOLS, SYMBOLS AND TALISMANS

Because each sephirah is first perceived as a set of concepts or principles, the assignment of perceptible objects adds an important dimension to it. Perceptible objects help to give each abstract idea a concrete form, and by doing so, make the intangible tangible. The attributes include: colours, gems, scents, plants, flowers, creatures, chemical elements, drugs and medicines, and the Tarot cards.

A group of magical tools and symbols also functions like a type of shorthand to signify the principles of the sephirah. The attributes, tools and symbols act as subtle reminders to the subconscious mind, and thereby reinforce the Qabalistic principles they represent. Used and valued cross-culturally since ancient times, practitioners often wear these in the form of talismans or amulets – objects or images such as the equal-armed cross, pyramid, triangle, five-, six- and seven-pointed stars and the like, which are thought to provide the wearer with protection and power. Several examples of attributes, magical tools, symbols and talismans follow.

Yellow, the colour assigned to Beauty, means to shimmer and to glow. This colour is a good match since Beauty is both the sphere of the Sun and home of the heart. The Sun shimmers and glows in the heavens and when our hearts are open we do likewise. Yellow (especially the golden hues) is the colour of autumn, and therefore the colour of ripeness linking it with the mature state of awareness symbolized by this sephirah.

The pearl is the gem linked with Understanding. The creation of a pearl requires numerous layers of work and so does Understanding. Also like Understanding, host and womb of the world, pearls are hosted in the oyster's womb-like body. In ancient times pearl divers believed each pearl had a soul, and Understanding is the sephirah wherein the soul is given to each incarnating body.

The myrtle tree is attributed to Victory, because its leaves and blue-black berries were made into wreaths for the winners in the ancient Olympic games.

The horse is assigned to Mercy. Mercy transports and conveys the universal truths and teachings from the sephiroth above much in the way that the horse is a vehicle of transport. Mercy represents an elevated level of human awareness, and the placement of someone upon a horse is a sign of elevation to a high or divine status.

Corn is the medicine or drug linked with Kingdom. When starvation becomes an illness, corn becomes the medicine that heals, whereas the drug-like properties of this plant may be

TABLE OF ATTRIBUTES

Sephirah	Colour	Gem	Scent	Plant/Tree Flower	Creatures	Drugs/ Medicines	Planets and Elements
The Crown	White	Diamond	Ambergris	Lotus Banyan	Hawk Swan	Elixir Vitae	Neptune Primordial Water
Wisdom	Grey	Star Ruby Turquoise	Musk Civet	Amaranth Pipal and Bo	Owl Eagle	Cocaine	Uranus Uranium
Understanding	Black	Pearl	Myrrh	Lily Cypress	Dove Pelican Sparrow	Soma	Saturn Lead
Mercy	Blue	Sapphire Lapis Lazuli Amethyst	Cedar	Pine Olive	Horse Unicorn	Opium	Jupiter Aluminium
Severity	Red	Ruby	Tobacco Flower	Stinging Nettle Cactus, Hickory	Wolf Dragon Basilisk	Caffeine	Mars Steel and Iron
Beauty	Yellow	Topaz Yellow Diamond	Olibanum	Gorse Acacia Oak	Lion Spider Phoenix	Alcohol	Sun Gold
Victory	Green	Emerald	Rose Sandalwood	Rose Laurel Myrtle	Raven Leopard Lynx	Sugar Cannabis Indica Anhalonium Lewinni	Venus Copper
Splendour	Orange	Fire Opal	Benzoin Storax	Moly	Jackal Monkey	LSD, MDMA Cannabis Indica Anhalonium Lewinni	Mercury Quicksilver
Foundation	Purple	Quartz Crystal	Jasmine	Alder Banyan	Elephant Tortoise	Ginseng, Mandrake Damiana Yohimba	Moon Silver
Kingdom	Earthy	Diamond in Matrix	Patchouli	Weeping Willow	Goat	Corn	Earth, Fire Water, Air

seen in corn whiskey. Like the human race, corn must be cultivated in order to grow properly. Corn is further associated with Kingdom because it requires cross-pollination, as does the earth's vegetation.

The sword and spear are magical tools that represent the sharp, cutting and piercing actions of Severity which operate in the name of divine service or tyranny. These weapons remind us of the importance of using discrimination and good judgement when enacting the powers of this sephirah.

The veil is a potent symbol for Foundation since this sephirah represents 'the veil', or boundary separating the world of the living from the world of the dead. A shroud is often used to cover or veil the deceased, an ancient sign showing that the deceased has 'crossed the veil' into the spirit realm. Individuals with 'second' or psychic insight, a quality of Foundation, are said to be born with a veil, part of the amnion, over their face.

A circle with a dot in the middle is a talisman of Wisdom. The unlimited life power, the dot or Crown sephirah, creates all that comes into the world of existence, the circle.

IMAGES OF ETERNITY

In addition to the Tarot cards, which will be discussed shortly, modern Qabalists created ten images to represent the sephiroth. This was done for much the same reason that various colours, gems, etc have been assigned to each sephirah. A picture presents us with something 'real' to contemplate and learn from. Although these images are not usually drawn, but rather merely referred to, they are simple enough to be easily imagined. However, if you are industrious and artistic, you might find it both enjoyable and insightful to transform these mental images into pictures.

Contemplating the image of a mighty crowned and throned monarch associated with Mercy gave me some valuable insights about the principle. The crown suggests that the ruler is connected with the heavens, the Crown sephirah. While ruling the earth, the sephirah of Kingdom, signified by the throne, the monarch is filled with the might and loving-kindness of the Most High. This image also brought to mind thoughts about the ancient practice of rulership by divine right which is relevant to the sphere of Mercy. First, the ruler was believed to be God's earthly representative and was ultimately only responsible to God for his/her actions. Second, the person who rules and lives his/her life according to this principle does what is both fair and merciful, despite the fact that his/her behaviours might be interpreted otherwise.

IMAGES ASSOCIATED WITH THE TEN SEPHIROTH OF THE TREE OF LIFE

The Crown/Kether:
An ancient one seen in profile.

Wisdom/Chokmah:
A bearded male figure.

Understanding/Binah:
A mature woman.

Mercy/Chesed:
A mighty crowned and throned monarch.

Severity/Geburah:
A warrior in a chariot.

Beauty/Tiphareth:
A child. A majestic monarch. A sacrificed god.

Victory/Netzach:
A beautiful naked woman.

Splendour/Hod:
A hermaphrodite.

Foundation/Yesod:

A very strong man (such as Atlas), traditionally beautiful and naked.

Kingdom/Malkuth:

A young woman crowned and throned. A bride.

THE TAROT AND THE QABALISTIC TREE OF LIFE

Although the Tarot cards have been discredited by those who see them only as a fortune-telling device, the Tarot is perhaps the most potent pictorial representation existing of the principles of the Qabalah.

The Universal Mind flows through thirty-two pathways or channels on the Tree of Life and becomes different states of consciousness. The ten sephiroth are the first ten paths, while the remaining twenty-two pathways flow between the sephiroth (Figure 5). Each of the twenty-two paths corresponds to one of the twenty-two letters in the Hebrew alphabet and to one of the twenty-two cards of the Tarot's Major Arcana. Qabalists consider the Major Arcana to be depictions of universal and natural laws and principles induced from the meaning of each Hebrew letter.

The sephiroth are also known as 'Gates', and the Tarot Cards as 'Keys'. This implies that Tarot Keys are used to unlock the mysteries of the Gates of the various sephiroth, or gateways to higher awareness.

FINDING YOUR WAY

To find your way along the paths of the Tree of Life, it eventually becomes necessary to have an in-depth working knowledge of the sacred language of the Hebrew letters. Learning the letters may be achieved by studying the pictures of the Tarot's Major Arcana. With proper guidance, they can be understood as one and the same (see *Living the Tarot*[1]).

The Minor Arcana, comprised of both the Court cards or Royalty, and number or Pip cards of the four Tarot suits, are paired up with the sephiroth according to their numbers and corresponding functions. Aces relate to the number one sephirah, the Crown; twos and kings with the number two sephirah, Wisdom; threes and queens with the number three sephirah, Understanding, and so on.

Although the twenty-two Major Arcana cards are directly linked with the twenty-two pathways, they are not usually linked with the first ten sephiroth. However, ten of these cards are associated with the ten planets, and the ten sephiroth have planetary attributes. For the sake of study, each sephirah may be astrologically coupled with one of the Tarot's Major Arcana. While this method duplicates ten of the cards already on the paths, it has proven itself to be helpful.

Sephiroth	Tarot Cards	Planet
(Paths 1-10)	Major and Minor Arcana	
One: The Crown	Hanged-man/Aces	Neptune (Traditionally, the entire universe)
Two: Wisdom	Fool/Twos/Kings	Uranus (Traditionally, the zodiac)
Three: Understanding	World/Threes/Queens	Saturn
Knowledge	Judgement	Pluto[2] (Minor Arcana cards are not assigned)
Four: Mercy	Wheel of Fortune/Fours	Jupiter
Five: Severity	Tower/Fives	Mars
Six: Beauty	Sun/Sixes/Knights	Sun
Seven: Victory	Empress/Sevens	Venus
Eight: Splendour	Magician/Eights	Mercury
Nine: Foundation	High Priestess/Nines	Moon
Ten: Kingdom	Devil[3] Tens/Pages	Earth

Please refer back to Figure 1 in order to see where the Major Arcana cards are placed.

Sephiroth

Paths 11–32	Tarot Cards
11	Fool
12	Magician
13	High Priestess
14	Empress
15	Emperor
16	Hierophant
17	Lovers
18	Chariot
19	Strength
20	Hermit
21	Wheel of Fortune
22	Justice
23	Hanged-Man
24	Death
25	Temperance
26	Devil
27	Tower
28	Star
29	Moon
30	Sun
31	Judgement
32	World

TAROT CARDS UPON THE PATHS

The primary difference between a sephirah and a path is that a sephirah represents a stage of evolutionary development, while a path is the personal experience one has when moving from one sephirah, or level of awareness, to another. Each path also signifies a check and balance point between the sephiroth it connects. Several illustrations of this principle follows.

The Death card, which in addition to physical death means spiritual rebirth, occupies the path between Victory, human desire and emotion, and Beauty, the sphere associated with the fully conscious personality. Death's placement shows us that certain desires naturally die off as we become increasingly Self-aware. Strength, indicating the loving restraint of our animal impulses, mediates the spheres of Mercy and Severity. This beautiful card illustrates the type of attitude needed to harmonize these potent qualities in our lives. Finally, the Tower card depicting the force that moves stagnant energy, eliminates misconceptions and opens the way to constructive criticism, spans the pathway between Victory, human emotion, and Splendour, intellect. Also called the Arousing Intelligence, this Tower depicts the upheaval that restores us when we are emotionally or mentally out of balance.

THE MINOR ARCANA

Here are some examples of how the principles of the Qabalah may be used to improve your Tarot skills.

The four sevens of the Tarot's Minor Arcana are associated with Victory, the sephirah most often associated with human feelings, desires and creative imagination. Looking carefully at these cards (Waite Tarot), we can see the internal and external struggles engendered by what we feel drawn to accomplish, conquer, wish for, create and express in picture form.

Working with these cards it is helpful to recall that taking immediate action upon blinding and/or primitive urges, passions, fantasies, drives and emotions may prove to be a disastrous initiation into the sphere of Victory in the short run. Yet these same behaviours foster our development over time.

In other words, Victory is called the Hidden Intelligence, and hidden within each card of this suit lies the opportunity for us to reach up the Tree of Life for the insight and inspiration to more clearly evaluate what we feel, rather than being influenced solely by the lower world of unclarified automatic reactions.

Briefly, the Seven of Wands implies the Victory of being able to manage our emotions in the face of adversity. The Seven of Cups suggests that although obscured, all of our desires originate from on high. The card also illustrates the truth that it is through our sense pleasures and physical experience that we eventually are spiritually refined. The Seven of Swords hints at the success possible when we refrain from making impulsive decisions. Despite the emotional discomfort involved, it is often more worthwhile to take up causes and projects which are suited to our temperament and abilities, than those which are not and are therefore best left behind. The Seven of Pentacles depicts us in our role as co-creators, and how we, by the fact of our humanness, are bound to work in harmony with universal and natural law. Therefore, when seeking to grow a wish or dream in the garden of our lives, we will achieve the greatest fulfilment by remembering to factor the universal and natural time frames into our personal equation for success. (Barring some miracle, blueberries will not grow in your front yard in January when you live in Helena, Montana.)

THE COURT CARDS

The four kings (Waite Tarot) wear crowns, indicating the divine authority that comes to Wisdom from the Crown, the Supreme Spirit that reigns over all. (Since the Qabalistic image of Wisdom is that of a bearded male figure, each king should ideally wear a beard.) While it is certain that the four kings are male, they may also signify the male or active aspect of a female's psyche (known in Jungian terms as the animus), or a female who has more of a male than female orientation to life.

Depending upon factors such as its placement in a Tarot spread, the question being asked of the kings, queens, knights and pages may either refer to oneself, one's client, or another person entirely. Generally, I look at the cards as the many facets of the subject – traits that are being enacted or are seeking enactment. Therefore, I am inclined to interpret these cards as the individual themselves, unless very clearly directed by my intuition to do otherwise.

When his ego does not supersede his higher Self, the King of Wands symbolizes a particularly inspired, and therefore inspirational and well-respected individual. He may signify the natural born leader who is strict, yet enacts rules that are for the greater good of those he leads. The King of Wands is a person who 'walks his talk', and searches his soul before acting. While the King of Wands often denotes someone who brings his Wisdom to the world, he may also be someone who has withdrawn from the outer world for insight and inspiration.

The King of Cups is a highly sensitive and receptive man who is devoted to carrying out the will of the Most High in all aspects of his life. He is imaginative, creative and successful at what he undertakes, especially when exercising his accumulated wisdom to lovingly direct his emotional impulses. The King of Cups may experience many emotional ups and downs. Although he might prefer not being tied down, he does complete what he commits himself to. Endowed with a well-developed social conscience, the King of Cups often denotes someone with humanitarian tendencies.

The King of Swords expresses the Divine will to act – the heaven-sent impetus to analyse and, when necessary, change internal states and external circumstances. He is someone who confidently eliminates distraction by enacting the powers of concentration and self-discipline. The King of Swords characterizes a dispassionate man who is reasonable, cooperation-oriented

and just. He not only aligns his actions with universal law, but can be in charge of assisting others to do likewise. His self-disciplined and intellectual nature disposes him to both scholarship and spiritual inquiry that are aimed at achieving a more well-balanced life and improved human relationships.

The King of Pentacles is intoxicated by the glory of the Most High manifest in the world around him. Because he is innately receptive to Wisdom, he has dominion over life, instead of the reverse. The ability to bring ideas into manifest form is natural to him. As someone who is attuned to the cosmic order, the King of Pentacles is able to penetrate the veil of illusion and perceive the true nature of the physical world. It is for this reason that he may represent a sensual individual who is deeply pleasured by the beauty of physical form and the holiness that lies within and behind it. The King of Pentacles may represent someone with a long-term commitment to the health and welfare of all on earth.

PATH WORK

Path Work is an advanced and involved practice. For the best results, it should be done with a comprehensive knowledge of the Qabalistic Tree of Life in all of its aspects. This includes the paths via their respective Hebrew letters or Tarot cards, the divine and angelic names, the Qabalistic Intelligences and Images, the attributes, magical tools and talismans, and the like.

ASTROLOGY, THE TREE OF LIFE AND US

Knowledge of the principles of the Qabalah may broaden our understanding of astrology because each sphere of the Tree of Life has an astrological correlation. Those who are already familiar with the principles of astrology find that study of the Tree of Life makes them more skilled.

For example, although the Crown sephirah is linked with the entire universe, it is also coupled with Neptune. Neptune is god of the oceans, and the Crown is the great cosmic ocean of unmanifest life that washes all of creation onto the shores of the manifest world. Neptune is considered the planet of inspiration, as the Crown is the inspiration for all life. Neptune presents an interesting paradox. Like the Crown, Neptune is the mystical consciousness that rules the dimensions above and beyond the physical plane. Yet, this same mystical consciousness ends up having ultimate dominion over the physical plane.

Saturn is the planet associated with the sphere of Understanding. Many astrologers associate Saturn with one's mother in the astrological chart. Qabalists link this planet with both our physical mother who gives us life, and our spiritual mother, who gives life to the entire world. The sphere of Understanding is the 'root of form', and Saturn is the power which crystallizes and condenses energy into form – the Great Mother turns the Great Father's energy into physical bodies. In order to have material form, there must be a boundary imposed upon infinite possibilities. Again, Understanding places a limited terrestrial construct upon the free-flowing potential of Wisdom. Saturn is equated with time and its restrictive nature, in much the same way as this sephirah is associated with the biological time of earthly life and the restrictions characteristic of the physical world.

THE SMALL WORLD REFLECTS THE GREAT WORLD

The Tree of Life, like astrology, is the study of the influence of the stars or cosmos upon human affairs. The Talmud mentions that the Patriarch Abraham practised astrology while living in Ur. Astrology, like the Tree of Life, suggests that 'All events are tied together in an unbroken wholeness'. This is summed by the Qabalistic principles 'microcosm-macrocosm', the small world reflects the great world, and 'As above, so below, as below, so above'.

We on earth are made of the same elements as the stars and planets. It is for these reasons that Qabalistic astrologers term the first seven or inner planets the seven inner stars – the Western counterpart to the Eastern chakra system. As noted, the remaining three planets, Uranus, Neptune, and Pluto, known as the outer planets, are also placed upon the Tree. These relatively new assignments are not meant to replace the more traditional correspondences, only to expand upon them.

The planets function within us like the planets in the heavens. Therefore, the assignment of a planet to each sephirah signifies: 1) the planet's *internal* operation or how it influences our temperament and well-being; and 2) the ways in which the movements of the planets have a natural and meaningful relationship to the events on earth and the universe that surrounds us. (The astrological correlations are listed in the table on page 115.)

SHAPES AND NUMBERS: SACRED GEOMETRY AND NUMEROLOGY

The Greek philosopher, Pythagoras, founded the Pythagorean mystery school in the sixth century BC. The Pythagoreans are best known for two principles: transmigration of souls, also known as reincarnation, and the theory that numbers constitute the true nature of things. According to Pythagoras, 'Everything is ordered according to the numbers'. Beginning with the discovery that the relationships between musical notes could be expressed in numerical ratios, the Pythagoreans devised an intricate and mystical theory of numbers. In brief, they taught that all things were numbers, meaning that the essential nature of physical forms was number. This also meant that everything – even abstract concepts like peace, anger, fear and love – could be expressed numerically.

The Pythagoreans also proposed that numbers *limit* the *unlimited*. This idea suggests a viable relationship between the Qabalistic Tree of Life, as it finitizes the infinite by way of numbers and the symbolic shapes they signify. The *Sefer Yetzirah*, or Book of Formation or Creation, appearing in the fifth century, shows the Most High creating the universe by means of the Hebrew alphabet in which each letter is given a numerical value. By combining the sacred letters with the sacred numbers and rearranging them in an endless array of configurations, Qabalists could bypass their intellects and the ordinary meaning of words and enter into an altered state of consciousness and understanding. This practice is termed the Magical Language or Gematria.

In the study of symbolism, numbers represent principles and natural forces. Like the Crown, the number one sephirah on the Tree of Life, representing the source of all, all numbers spring from the number one. Many numerologists believe that the further a number is from one, the more it is involved in the process of physical evolution. Conversely, the closer a number is to one, the more involved it is in the process of spiritual evolution and the concepts that accompany it. These ideas are substantiated by the way in which the ten sephiroth of Tree of Life are ordered. When sequenced from one through ten, the sephiroth illustrate the process of involution – spirit becoming matter, yet when this sequence is reversed, it shows the process of evolution – matter, returning to spirit.

SEPHIROTH, SHAPES AND NUMBERS

The following is a general outline of the attributes applied to the numbers one through ten (Figure 6). This outline may also be seen as a sketch of the ten sephiroth.

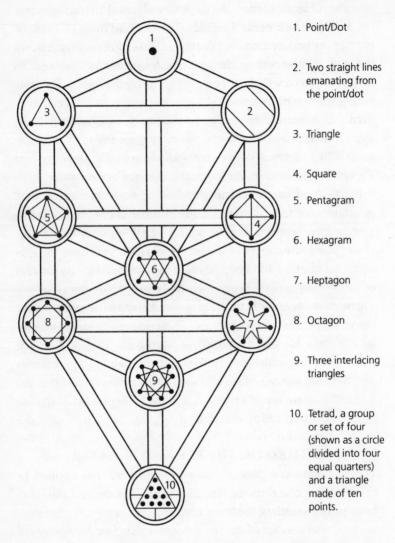

1. Point/Dot

2. Two straight lines emanating from the point/dot

3. Triangle

4. Square

5. Pentagram

6. Hexagram

7. Heptagon

8. Octagon

9. Three interlacing triangles

10. Tetrad, a group or set of four (shown as a circle divided into four equal quarters) and a triangle made of ten points.

Figure 6 The geometric shapes and numbers that correlate to the Qabalistic Tree of Life.

One:　Geometrically, one is symbolized by the point or dot. One is the mystic centre, the indivisible point of no dimension, the point of emanation and supreme power. This number is equated with spiritual unity or oneness – the common thread that runs between everything in the manifest world. Number one is further linked with light. All this certainly describes many qualities of the first sephirah, the Crown!

Two:　Geometrically, two is symbolized by two points or dots, two lines or an angle. The one-dimensional line signifies the passage of time, the line which progresses forward from its point of origination. Number two symbolizes the ideas of duality and reflection as well as those of the echo, shadow, and the momentary stillness that occurs when two forces are in balance. Much like activities of the second sephirah, Wisdom, two is regarded as a reflection of the immortal and a step forward in the process of physical manifestation.

Three:　Geometrically, three is symbolized by three points or dots and the two-dimensional triangle. It is the ternary or what consists of three. Three suggests the trinity, triple goddess (birth, life and death), and the formula for creation and synthesis. This number also stands for the resolution to the conflict posed by duality, because three is considered the product of the action of unity upon duality, as it is in the activities of the third sephirah, Understanding.

Four:　Geometrically, four is symbolized by four points or dots, the square (a flat four-sided figure), and the cross representing the four points of the compass, elements and seasons of nature. The cross signifies the descent of spirit into matter, and ascent of matter into spirit, as does the fourth sephirah, Mercy. To Pythagoreans, four is the quaternary, what consists of four. This number represents stability, the earth and its inhabitants, rational organization, tangible effects and what is three dimensional.

Five: Geometrically, five is symbolized by five points or dots, the pentagram (a flat five-sided figure) or five-pointed star, a symbol that has long been attributed to the human race – the points are our head and four limbs. Because the number five falls in the middle of the sequence of single-digit numbers one through nine, five suggests how each human being serves as a mediator between the material and spiritual worlds. Five is also linked with the five senses, through which we may learn to perceive the spirit in the world around us. It is the number of higher truth and the voice of our conscience or intuition. Like the principles of the fifth sephirah, Severity, five shows that although living truthfully may be difficult in the short run, it is not nearly as severe as the effects or repercussions of failing to abide by truth.

Six: Geometrically, six is symbolized by six points or dots, the hexagram (a flat six-sided figure or two interlacing triangles). The hexagram is composed of two triangles that signify the mystical union of fire and water and the sacred marriage of the masculine and feminine principles. This number further corresponds to the six directions of space and the cessation of movement or stillness at a central point. Like the sixth sephirah, Beauty, six is equated with equilibrium, inner peace, love and harmony.

Seven: Geometrically, seven is symbolized by seven points or dots, the heptagon (a flat seven-sided figure). Because the seven-pointed star is made by combining the triangle or ternary and the square or quaternary, it suggests the alignment of heaven and earth. Seven refers to the basic series of musical notes, the seven colours of the rainbow, the first seven planets which correspond to the seven chakras, and the seven sins and seven virtues, which are linked with what we desire. This number also indicates a finished cycle, end of a time period, fulfilment, celebration, and a victorious conclusion. The name of the seventh sephirah is Victory. Victory is associated with our desires and passions and how their fulfilment serves to elevate our consciousness.

Eight: Geometrically, eight is symbolized by eight points or dots, an octagon (a flat eight-sided figure comprised of two interlacing squares), and the Pythagorean octonary. This number and the actual shape of the number itself, is often equated with interdependence and interconnection and the Principle of Correspondence: 'As above, so below', and vice versa. Eight further suggests the eternally spiralling movement of the heavens, order and the power that the human intelligence may exert over itself and matter. It is aligned with the eighth sephirah, Splendour, linked with the human mind.

Nine: Geometrically, nine is symbolized by nine points or dots, the triangle of the ternary or the triplication of the triple (three three-sided and flat interlacing triangles). Nine is a number of assimilation, separate elements combined to create a whole, and completion, as it is the end of the numerical series before its return to unity or transformation into a new form. Paired with the ninth sephirah, Foundation, nine stands for the assimilation of our life experiences which enables our thoughts, words and deeds to be automatically based upon higher truth and universal principles.

Ten: Geometrically, ten is symbolized by ten points or dots or the decad, a decagon (a flat ten-sided figure that may be comprised of two interlacing pentagrams), a triangle comprised of ten points and the tetrad. This number is also depicted by the ten-sided double cube. Ten signifies spiritual and physical achievement (which may be seen as one and the same) and new beginnings. Ten is equated with the spiritual world brought into manifest form, as is the tenth sephirah, Kingdom. Finally, from the most ancient of times ten has been used to symbolize perfection as it reduces (1+0=1) back to the number one, or the One.

GODS AND GODDESSES: MYTHOLOGY AND THE QABALISTIC TREE OF LIFE

The ancient practice of ascribing human characteristics to non-human beings, objects, natural phenomena, principles or ideas and concepts, known as anthropomorphism, is another valuable way to become acquainted with the Qabalistic Tree of Life. This can potentially help us to identify these qualities and principles within ourselves. For instance, if by learning about the goddess Venus, a man becomes more aware of his feelings, he is also becoming more aware of the principles of the seventh sephirah, Victory, linked with the planet Venus upon the Tree of Life.

Because all comes from the One, Qabalists are able to address the Most High by many names and to acknowledge the various pagan pantheons. Yet, to those who believe in 'one God', the assignment of various pagan pantheons to the Qabalistic Tree of Life is blasphemous. With thought, such believers may learn to open their minds and realize the value of adding the dimension of polytheism, the belief in many gods, to monotheism or the belief in one God. In other words, if the sephiroth are aspects or emanations of the One, why not consider the various deities who, in most mythologies, are said to *originate* from one or another neutral, genderless, self-created and self-sustaining primary creator deity, in the same light?

The application of many gods to what was once a strictly one God system demonstrates how the *Universal* Tree of Life brings the Eastern and Western religio-spiritual traditions together. For instance, while the fifth sephirah, Severity, represents the forceful, fierce, angry and no-nonsense aspect of the Most High, additional insight may be gained by contemplating Severity in relationship to the Buddhist Vajrapani as well as Rudra, the earliest form of Shiva, Ares and Mars.

Although neither gods nor goddesses, I will sometimes add people to these listings. Solomon, king of the ancient Hebrews, is an excellent example of Mercy. Marilyn Monroe fits in with Victory, the sphere most associated with passion and physical beauty.

THE GRADED TREE OF LIFE

The Graded Tree of Life is a remnant of the ancient mystery schools of Egypt and Greece. This system was created to show how spiritual development through these traditions progresses, and to provide a general plan for the student's own aspirations. Because each grade has specific characteristics and proficiencies, it gives the seeker both an internal and external means of measuring progress.

Predictably, this turned into a form of childish spiritual one-upmanship – 'Na, Na, Na, Na, Na! I'm a Theoricus and you're only a Zelator!' Putting this pitfall aside, the Graded Tree of Life offers another way to grasp the aspect of human evolution possible through the mastery of each sephirah. In order to understand the workings of the Graded Tree, ideally one should be

CORRESPONDENCES BETWEEN THE SEPHIROTH AND VARIOUS PANTHEONS

Sephirah	Egyptian	Greek	Roman	Hindu	Scandinavian
The Crown	Osiris	Zeus	Jupiter	Parabrahma	Ymir
Wisdom	Thoth	Athena	Janus	Vishnu	Odin
Understanding	Isis	Dictynna	Ops	Ma Shakti	Frigg
Mercy	Amoun	Poseidon	Neptune	Indra	Thor
Severity	Set	Ares	Mars	Shiva	Loki
Beauty	Ra	Apollo	Helios	Aditi	Balder
Victory	Hathor	Aphrodite	Venus	Saraswati	Freija
Splendour	Anubis	Hermes	Mercury	Hanuman	Bragi
Foundation	Shu	Hecate	Diana	Ganesh	Hel
Kingdom	Geb	Gaia	Ceres	Lakshmi	Nerthus

open to a belief in reincarnation, for without it, the multi-levelled process outlined becomes difficult, if not impossible, to fathom.

Because the spiritual evolution of the ordinary human being into the extraordinary human being starts at the bottom of the Tree of Life in Kingdom, so does the system of ascending grades. Much like our physical development, this is a *natural* process that all of us go through, whether we are cognizant of it or not. In many cases, awareness initially creates angst, yet as we become increasingly developed, we relax and become less anxious about our progress. This is because our perspective has expanded to include the certainty that growth is not only inevitable, but that it happens in divine time, not ours.

A NATURAL PROCESS

All of us begin our spiritual journey at the base of the Tree of Life as Zelators in Kingdom. In time, we naturally evolve our way up the Tree of Life to the enlightened Lesser and Greater Adepts associated with Beauty and Severity. An example of this process is seen in the transformation of prince Siddhartha Gautama into the Buddha. After reaching this grade and level of consciousness, we may, at death, opt to sever all earthly ties and personal identifications to return to the source of life symbolized by the Crown. Or, we may also *choose* to be reborn but in an exalted state. That is, we reenter this world at the elevated level at which we exited. Within the Western mystery schools such persons are known as Exempt Adepts.

In summary, we experience *all* levels or grades of consciousness before we achieve the grade of the Exempt Adept. The Lesser and Greater Adepts are born as ordinary people, but through the natural process of spiritual maturation achieve enlightenment – also termed Super-consciousness, Self-Realization, Satori, Nirvana, Christ-consciousness or Buddhahood. Having reached this level, one may either rejoin the Most High in the first sphere of the

Crown, or again descend into the human race. Exempt Adepts are those enlightened beings who, at death, elect to take up another physical body in order to return to the physical world to ease suffering. These individuals have paid their personal karmic debts, yet remain subject to worldly, socio-economic and political karma such as diseases and natural disasters, racism, sexism and war.

EXTRAORDINARY SOULS

The Exempt Adepts are those extraordinary souls who have purposefully retaken a human form to assist in the administration of universal law, love and truth, and by doing so contribute to the evolution of human consciousness and healing of the world around them. While it is true that this group may include prominent personalities, the majority of these people are not motivated by the desire for personal public recognition – such may be a result of what they do, but it is *not* the cause.

Contrary to popular belief, persons of this type are not always 'healers and spiritual teachers' per se, but those who dedicate their lives to serving humanitarian ideals and causes. In essence, they have a deep reverence for the sanctity of all life. For this reason, their activities may take the form of adopting children with AIDS or similar conditions; setting up a neighbourhood soup kitchen; feeding and/or immunizing stray animals; refusing to abide by racist laws; doing the legal work required to file a class-action lawsuit against a business that discriminates against lesbians and gays in its hiring policies; volunteering to tend a sick or elderly neighbour; mentoring a fatherless boy or motherless girl, or some other type of work that inadvertently wins public acclaim. In other words, individuals assume whatever role that will best help them to accomplish their life purpose.

The word Zelator is derived from zeal and means enthusiasm and devotion. As the first grade, the Zelator has undergone a spiritual awakening and is excited. He/she is busy talking about his/her transformation and how important it is to have a spiritual practice *exactly* like his/hers. This system is so well thought out that the title of this grade also warns against one of the grade's major pitfalls, that of becoming a Zealot, someone who is fanatical about his/her beliefs. (Does this description sound familiar?)

The terms theorist and theoretician, one who is a student of theories or principles, may be interchanged with the title Theoricus. The Theoricus is focused on getting acquainted with the basic spiritual theories or principles that will support his/her development. The word Theoricus is also related to the word theorem, a mathematical term used to specify a proven concept. This tells us that the Theoricus is willing to let go of ways of thinking and behaving that have been proven to be incorrect or outdated.

THE GRADED TREE OF LIFE IN ASCENDING ORDER

Sphere	Grade
Kingdom	Zelator
Foundation	Theoricus
Splendour	Practicus
Victory	Philosophus
Beauty	Lesser Adept
Severity	Greater Adept
Mercy	Exempt Adept
Understanding	Master of the Temple
Wisdom	Magus
The Crown	Ipsissimus

IN THE NAME OF HEAVEN

Divine and archangelic presences are believed to reign over each of the ten sephiroth on the Qabalistic Tree of Life. Learning about the angelic and divine presences linked with a sephirah is both fascinating and aids our understanding. For example, the archangel assigned to Mercy is Tzadkiel. Tzadkiel, the agent of divine Mercy, is believed to have held back the Patriarch Abraham's arm just at the moment he was about to sacrifice his son, Isaac. The aspect of the divine presence assigned to Mercy is El. El is referred to throughout the Bible's Book of Job to emphasize Job's faith in the Mercy of the Most High and to show how Job drew his strength from this 'God of Strength' throughout his trials and tribulations. A good dictionary of angels or a religious encyclopaedia, available at most libraries, will help you with this intriguing process.

WORDS OF POWER

Invoking or calling up a particular divine or angelic name invites that presence into our lives. Because these holy words, known as Words of Power, vibrate at higher frequencies than ordinary language, they enable us to become better receiving stations for the energies from on high. In this way, the practice of invocation tunes us into the energies of a sephirah so that we may more easily grasp and apply its principles.

ANGELS AND MAGICAL NAMES

The word 'angel' originates from the Greek *angelos*, and the Hebrew *mal'akh*, meaning messenger. There are two types of angels. Some perform a holy mission, such as delivering a message or prophecy from the godhead to an individual or group, carrying out sacred decrees, recording events, guiding and protecting the world of creation, and bearing the souls of the dead to heaven. The second type of angels are members of the heavenly court who surround and praise the Most High (Isaiah 6:1–7). Angels are mentioned in the Old Testament's Books of Ezekiel and Zechariah as well as in the New Testament, Apocrypha, *Koran* and *Bhagavad Gita*.

Writings of the thirteenth century mystic, Eleazar of Worms, concerning the names of angels and the magical names of the Most High are said to be the earliest works known as Kabbalah. He states that the Qabalah and Tree of Life were given to humanity by the angels. Because the word Qabalah is translated from the Hebrew to mean 'to receive' and 'from mouth to ear', the Qabalah and Tree of Life are considered to be sacred revelations passed from the mouth of the Most High God to the human ear via the angels. Other Jewish mystics teach that the angelic hierarchy functions like a school. This heavenly body instructs and guides human souls through their evolutionary journey by way of a system of ascending grades which begins at the bottom of the Qabalistic Tree of Life.

TEN DIVINE PRESENCES AND THE ANGELIC ORDERS IN ASCENDING ORDER

Sphere: Kingdom
Divine Presence: *Adonai Melek*, 'The Most High in manifest form'
Archangel: Sandalphon, 'Sound of Sandals and Co-brother'
Hebrew Order: *Ashim*, Just Souls
Christian Order: Souls

Sphere: Foundation
Divine Presence: *Shaddai El Chai*, 'The Almighty living divine'
Archangel: Gabriel, 'Messenger of the Most High'
Hebrew Order: *Kerubim*, Souls of Fire
Christian Order: Angels

Sphere: Splendour
Divine Presence: *Elohim Tzabaoth*, 'Host of Hosts'
Archangel: Michael, 'Who is like the Most High'
Hebrew Order: *Beni Elohim*, Sons and Daughters of the Most High God,
Christian Order: Archangels

Sphere: Victory
Divine Presence: *Yahweh Tzabaoth*, 'Lord of Hosts'
Archangel: Uriel, 'Light of the Most High'
Hebrew Order: *Elohim*, Gods and Goddesses
Christian Order: Principalities

Sphere: Beauty
Divine Presence: *Yahweh Eloah Va Da'at*, 'God of Knowledge
and Reason'
Archangel: Raphael, 'Healer of the Most High'
Hebrew Order: *Malachim*, Messengers
Christian Order: Virtues

Sphere: Severity
Divine Presence: *Elohim Gebor*, 'The Almighty One'
Archangel: Khamael, 'Helper of the Most High'
Hebrew Order: *Seraphim*, Fiery Serpents
Christian Order: Powers

Sphere: Mercy
Divine Presence: *El*, 'God of Strength'
Archangel: Tzadkiel, 'Righteousness of the Most High'
Hebrew Order: *Chasmalim*, Brilliant Ones
Christian Order: Dominations

Sphere: Understanding
Divine Presence; *Elohim*, 'Mother Goddess, God of Gods'
Archangel: Tzaphkiel, 'Knowledge of the Most High'
Hebrew Order: *Aralim*, Thrones
Christian Order: Thrones

Sphere: Wisdom
Divine Presence: *Yahweh*, 'Father God', 'God of Gods'
Archangel: Ratziel, 'Bearer of The Word of the Most High'
Hebrew Order: *Auphanim*, Wheels
Christian Order: Cherubim

Sphere: The Crown
Divine Presence: *Eheyeh*, 'All that was, is, and will always be'
Archangel: Metatron, 'Instrument of the Most High'
Hebrew Order: *Chailoth ha Qadesh*, Holy Living Creatures
Christian Order: Seraphim

NOTES

1 *Living the Tarot*, Amber Jayanti (Llewellyn Publications, 1992).
2 Usually not included in the sephiroth, Knowledge or *Da'ath*, the 'invisible' sephirah, may be paired with both the Judgment card and the planet Pluto.
3 Although the Devil is linked with Capricorn, an earth sign, those who are knowledgeable about this card may see enough similarities between it and the planet Earth to find study useful.

FURTHER STUDY AND MEDITATION

UNIVERSAL QABALAH, A MYSTERY SCHOOL TRADITION

The Qabalah is considered to be one of the great mystery school traditions. Although a mystery is something that is secret, unexplained or unknown, these schools teach students the invaluable principle that 'nothing is secret from those who wish to know.'

What distinguishes a mystery school from others is that the student in a mystery school already has a *basic* understanding of right and wrong. Therefore, instead of being taught specifically what to do and what not to do, students are taught universal and natural laws and principles by which they learn to guide themselves. Learning takes place through the process of trial and error and through developing one's intuition and sense of discrimination. For example, knowledge of the Principle of Cause and Effect not only shows us that actions have results, it encourages us to consider what we say and do with care.

CLUES

The student, with the help of the clues or tools provided by his/her knowledge of principles, such as those in this book, a relationship with a teacher, and his/her inner teacher or intuition, learns how to solve the mysteries of life. This experience helps him/her to achieves self-mastery and higher consciousness. Perhaps the greatest mystery of the mystery school, is that the initiates must figure out the mysteries of life for themselves. No one genuinely knows what is best for another. This is one of the primary reasons that such traditions are not for those who are looking to be told exactly what to do and when to do it.

> A student recounted a story of a man who paid a very large sum of money for an hour of guidance from a prominent spiritual teacher. When, after carrying out the teacher's advice to the letter, his life did not improve, the man angrily blamed her rather than himself. In such instances, we not only give up our power by abdicating our role in the decision-making process, we also deny ourselves the growth and learning opportunities that the Principles of Free Will and Personal Responsibility provide.

WE BECOME WHO AND WHAT WE REALLY ARE

Another enigma of the Qabalistic mystery school tradition, is that each person evolves in his/her own way and according to his/her own timetable. What is right for one person is not right for another. What works at one point in life may not work at another. In the Qabalistic tradition, a pagan becomes a pagan, a Christian a Christian, a Jew a Jew, a Buddhist a Buddhist, and so forth. And beyond all of these identifications, we become who and what we *really* are. Therefore, the most important principle of the Qabalah is: Seek what is Real!

FOUR WAYS TO LEARN MORE ABOUT THE QABALAH

You may learn more about the Qabalah by: 1) reading and studying books such as this one, 2) working directly with a teacher, 3) listening to your intuition – the knowledge that comes through one's 'inner teacher' is usually an offshoot of the first two types of learning – and 4) taking the time to pray and meditate.

QABALISTIC PRAYER AND MEDITATION

Prayer and meditation help Qabalists to bridge the physical and spiritual worlds. Prayer is our expression of gratitude in addition to the heartfelt request for healing, blessing, guidance and understanding. Meditation is what we do with our mind and body to develop and maintain an intimate relationship with our higher Self and the infinite. These practices assist us to step from the personal into the transpersonal so that we may return to the personal able to see, hear, feel and comprehend more clearly.

Prayer and meditation enable us to temporarily bypass ordinary and obsolete ways of thinking and feeling in order to generate new ideas, find truth, peace, inspiration and make contact with our soul spirit Self. Qabalists know it is often necessary to lay aside our preconceptions about how things 'must or should be' in order to gain a better understanding of ourselves, others, world events, and the workings of the Most High.

QABALISTIC MEDITATION

The most common forms of meditation are those which focus on either a particular sephirah or the entire Tree of Life. The majority of techniques require some amount of regulated breathing and a heightened awareness of the universal life force or breath flowing in and out of the practitioner's body. In many

instances, these can also include visualizations, as well as the use of certain colours and scents. Another type of meditation, termed Gematria, centres on the sacred meaning of words and numbers. My favourite meditation invokes the divine and archangelic names, called Words of Power, via chanting. Qabalistic chanting or spoken repetition (mantra) is a very potent way to meditate upon the Tree of Life.

The Principle of Vibration tells us that everything moves and vibrates. Since each sephirah is linked with a divine and angelic presence, names of these presences or Words of Power vibrate at a higher frequency than ordinary words. When we chant or repeat them, we raise our personal level of vibration to this higher, impersonal level of vibration. Chanting also conveys more of this type of energy into the world around us. You may order a tape of sacred chants through the Santa Cruz School for Tarot and Qabalah Study listed in the Resource Guide at the end of this book.

As the principles of the Qabalah become integrated into our daily lives, the very act of doing mundane activities becomes an opportunity to interact with the divine and serves as a remarkably powerful meditation. Qabalistic meditation makes us increasingly conscious or mindful, so that we are able to be in this state, both when taking the 'time out' from life to meditate, and while engaging in our ordinary chores and activities. Because of this, the distinction between spiritual and worldly activities becomes less discernible and both we and our lives become more unified.

QABALISTIC YOGA POSTURES

There is also a systematic practice of physical postures that mirror the Hebrew alphabet known as *Ophanim*, meaning 'angels of form'. Akin to yoga, these meditational exercises balance and strengthen the body and forge a link between physical

and spiritual existence. Keep your eyes open for classes and books on this little known discipline.

LIVING THE TREE OF LIFE

While meditation and chanting are a wonderful part of Qabalah study, equally wondrous is living its teachings day to day.

The Tree of *Life* is about life, and I do not know anything more rewarding than applying its wisdom every day and watching how much life improves. In other words, it is one thing to know about the principles of Mercy and Severity and another to apply them to a situation in one's home or workplace. I am just completing an in-depth book on the Universal Qabalah that provides many examples of how my students and I do this very thing! Following is an example of how Ann, a sculptress and mother of two, applied the teachings of Severity to solve a problem.

'Most of my lesson with Severity came up a couple of days ago. My husband, Josh, is a great man, yet when it comes to dealing with our tenants, he's a great procrastinator. Before the lease on our rental property expired, we decided not to renew it with the current tenant. Josh kept saying, "I'll give him notice". But the days kept slipping by, and the time left to give him a legal thirty-day notice was to be up this past week.

'The tenant seems to prefer dealing with Josh. He avoids eye contact with me, and when he's spoken to me it's usually in an impatient and somewhat hostile tone. But, business needs to be done and so I decided to take it on because not doing so meant continued problems with his unkept yard, late rent and generally uncooperative and nasty attitude. Also, with the housing shortage in our area, Joshua and I had been talking about renting the house to a family.

'Before delivering the termination notice, I was feeling unsettled and decided I'd best ask for guidance and direction. So I turned to our work with Severity for inspiration. It was amazing. Not only did I muster my forces, or should I say, The Force of Severity, I also got the great idea to wear a suit of armour! I mentally created this outrageous golden chain mail, put a shield emblazoned with the Gorgon Medusa over my heart, topped my helmet with a scarlet plume and set out to give our tenant notice. I actually can't put into words how much doing this helped.

'I approached him with an assurance that I never quite felt before, handed him the notice, and thanked him for his cooperation. I definitely felt daggers and spears being thrown at my back as I walked away. But being protected by my armour, they just bounced off. The whole experience turned out to be empowering and energizing, rather than disempowering and exhausting. I can't deny that it wasn't a battle of sorts, but as it turned out it was more of a battle of me with myself than with him. I'm finding out that if I don't stand up for what I believe is right, I feel even more defeated. At least in this situation I knew what to expect, and thanks to the teachings of Severity, how to protect myself and take care of business at the same time.'

THE PATTERN ON THE TRESTLEBOARD

The Pattern on the Trestleboard was conceived by Paul Foster Case who was schooled in the Masonic, Rosicrucian and Qabalistic traditions. Case claimed to have received these statements in a state of deep meditation. The word 'pattern' means an original from which others are copied. Contained within the idea of a pattern is the concept of an ordered design or plan. The modern Qabalistic school is patterned after the Masonic and Rosicrucian orders. A trestleboard is an architect's drawing table. In Freemasonry, it denotes the place where the Grand Architect, the Order's name for the Most High God, draws out the plans for the universe.

The Pattern on the Trestleboard is a brief yet accurate explanation of each sephiroth's meaning and our place in the divine order. It outlines the ten aspects of the Most High, in the form of the ten sephiroth on the Tree of Life, in ten statements. Each affirmation-like statement is made personally relevant by including the words, 'I, me, my'.

Like the Tree of Life, *The Pattern on the Trestleboard* represents the Most High's plan for humanity. It is a blueprint of the way in which our human consciousness evolves until we realize our full potential – complete conscious identification with the godhead. You might find that repeating these lines daily will be a way of affirming your divine nature and place in scheme of things.

THE PATTERN ON THE TRESTLEBOARD

This is the truth about the Self:

All the power that ever was or will be is here now.

1 I am a centre of expression for the Primal Will-to-Good which eternally creates and sustains the universe.

2 Through me its unfailing Wisdom takes form in thought and word.

3 Filled with Understanding of its perfect law, I am guided, moment by moment, along the Path of Liberation.

4 From the exhaustless riches of Its Limitless Substance, I draw all things needful, both spiritual and material.

5 I recognize the manifestation of the undeviating Justice in all the circumstances of my life.

6 In all things, great and small, I see the Beauty of the divine expression.

7 Living from that Will, supported by its unfailing Wisdom and Understanding, mine is the Victorious Life.

8 I look forward with confidence to the perfect realization of the Eternal Splendour of the Limitless Light.

9 In thought and word and deed, I rest my life, from day to day, upon the sure Foundation of Eternal Being.

10 The realm of Spirit is embodied in my flesh.

RESOURCE GUIDE

The Fraternity of the Hidden Light
  PO Box 5094
  Covina, CA 91723

The Meru Foundation
  PO Box 503
  Sharon, Massachusettes 02067
  Telephone: 1 888 422 MERU
  Website: http://www.meru.org

Sancta Sophia Seminary
  Carol E. Parrish
  11 Summit Ridge Drive
  Tahlequah, Oklahoma 74464–9515
  Telephone: (800) 863 7161

Santa Cruz School for Tarot and Qabalah Study
  Amber Jayanti
  PO Box 1692
  Soquel, California 95073–1692
  Telephone: (831) 423 9742
  amber@practical–mystic.com
  http://practical–mystic.com

Servants of the Light
   Fran Keegan
   PO Box 6563
   Syracuse, New York 13217–6563
   keegan@aol.com

A Society of Souls
   Jason Schulman
   17 Witherspoon Ct
   Morristown, New Jersey 07960
   Telephone: (973) 538 7689

Thelemic Order of the Golden Dawn
   126 North Wilcox Avenue #481
   Los Angeles, CA 90028
   ordotgd@aol.com

GREAT BRITAIN

International Order of Kabbalists
   Send sae to:
   The Principles
   25 Circle Gardens
   Merton Park
   London SW19

OGDOS – Oxford Golden Dawn Occult Society
   PO Box 250
   Oxford OX1

Servants of the Light
   PO Box 215
   St Helier, Jersey
   Channel Islands JE4 9SD

The Toledo School of Kabalah
treelife@easynet.co.uk

AUSTRALIA

Servants of the Light
Laurel Ellis
PO Box 555
Bentley
Western Australia 6102
laurmile@inet.net.au

EUROPE

Servants of the Light
SOL Sweden
BOX 22818624 Vallentuna
solswe@algone.se

Z'ev ben Shimon Halevi (Warren Kenton)
Barcelona
Spain
qblh@wsite.es
Workshops are given throughout the world, including Australia, Japan, Europe and the UK.

ISRAEL

Bnei Baruch
PO Box 584
Bnei-Bral
51104 Israel
Information is available in Hebrew, French, Russian, Arabic, Portuguese and German.

Builders of the Adytum (BOTA)
USA and Europe
www.bota.org
Information is available in English, Spanish, French, German,
Dutch and Swedish.

Hermetic Order of the Golden Dawn
www.goldendawn.org

The Kabbalah Home Page
Website: http://kabbalah-web.org
Information is available in English, French, Russian, Italian,
Arabic, Spanish, Portuguese and German.